SQUADRONS!

No. 23

AF408580

THE REPUBLIC
THUNDERBOLT MK. II

PHIL H. LISTEMANN

ISBN: 979-1096490-18-9

Copyright

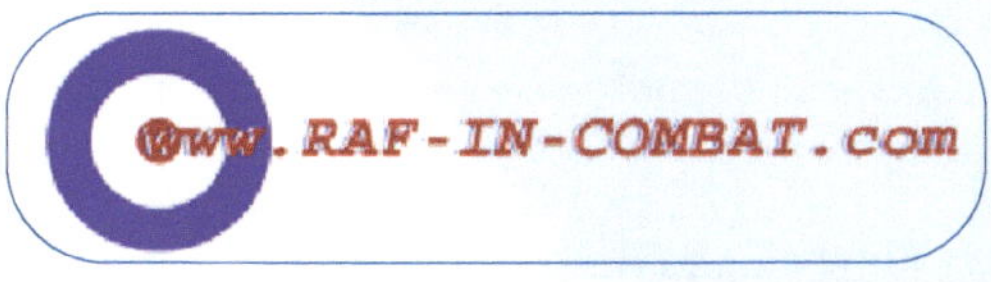

Colour profiles: Gaetan Marie/Bravo Bravo Aviation

GLOSSARY OF TERMS

PERSONEL :
(AUS)/RAF: Australian serving in the RAF
(BEL)/RAF: Belgian serving in the RAF
(CAN)/RAF: Canadian serving in the RAF
(CZ)/RAF: Czechoslovak serving in the RAF
(NFL)/RAF: Newfoundlander serving in the RAF
(NL)/RAF: Dutch serving in the RAF
(NZ)/RAF: New Zealander serving in the RAF
(POL)/RAF: Pole serving in the RAF
(RHO)/RAF: Rhodesian serving in the RAF
(SA)/RAF: South African serving in the RAF
(US)/RAF - RCAF : American serving in the RAF or RCAF

RANKS
G/C : Group Captain
W/C : Wing Commander
S/L : Squadron Leader
F/L : Flight Lieutenant
F/O : Flying Officer
P/O : Pilot Officer
W/O : Warrant Officer
F/Sgt : Flight Sergeant
Sgt : Sergeant
Cpl : Corporal
LAC : Leading Aircraftman

OTHER
ATA: Air Transport Auxiliary
CO : Commander
DFC : Distinguished Flying Cross
DFM : Distinguished Flying Medal
DSO : Distinguished Service Order
Eva. : Evaded
ORB : Operational Record Book
OTU : Operational Training Unit
PoW : Prisoner of War
PAF: Polish Air Force
RAF : Royal Air Force
RAAF : Royal Australian Air Force
RCAF : Royal Canadian Air Force
RNZAF : Royal New Zealand Air Force
SAAF : South African Air Force
s/d: Shot down
Sqn : Squadron
† : Killed

CODENAMES - OFFENSIVE OPERATIONS - FIGHTER COMMAND

CIRCUS:
Bombers heavily escorted by fighters, the purpose being to bring enemy figthers into combat.

RAMROD:
Bombers escorted by fighters, the primary aim being to destroy a target.

RANGER:
Large formation freelance intrusion over enemy territory with aim of wearing down enemy figthers.

RHUBARD:
Freelance fighter sortie against targets of opportunity.

RODEO:
A fighter sweep without bombers.

SWEEP:
An offensive flight by fighters designed to draw up and clear the enemy from the sky.

THE THUNDERBOLT II

In mid-1943, the RAF was facing a major challenge, as it needed to find a successor for two single-engine aircraft types, the Hawker Hurricane and the Curtiss Kittyhawk. Both were then being used with success as fighter-bombers, but at the same time both had reached the limits of their development. The Hurricane was employed in all major theatres - Europe, the Mediterranean and the Far East - while the Kittyhawk was only serving in the Mediterranean. In Europe, use of the Hurricane as a front-line aircraft had come to an end with the widespread introduction of the Typhoon. For the two other theatres – the Mediterranean and the Far East – the problem remained unresolved as the Typhoon proved unsuitable in hot climates. The Allies, meanwhile, were planning how to end the war. Whatever they decided upon, massive air offensives would play a major part.

When the tropical tests carried out with the Typhoon in North Africa in 1943 showed unsatisfactory results, other types needed to be considered. Only the Americans could help. Two US fighters were available at the time: the North American Mustang and the Republic Thunderbolt. As the USAAF was in the process of increasing its strength by adding to the number of fighter groups under its command, both types were reserved for USAAF units first. The RAF, therefore, could not obtain the desired quantity of aircraft, especially in the case of the Mustang for which the RAF had a clear preference. This was also true of the American forces, which was somewhat ironic considering the Mustang was an aircraft they did not want at first because its design hadn't been initiated by or for the USAAF. While the British were able to get some Mustangs for their squadrons, the number allocated was insufficient to re-equip all of the units so priorities were decided upon. The RAF needed long-range escort fighters, a task the Spitfire could not completely meet, so the UK-based Air Defence of Great Britain (ADGB) and 2nd Tactical Air Force (2 TAF) squadrons were given priority when it came to Mustangs. This left about a third of the allocations available for other theatres. As the threat posed by the Luftwaffe was considered to be greater than that of the Japanese air arms, the Mustangs not required for UK-based squadrons were sent to the Mediterranean where they began to re-equip the Kittyhawk squadrons. In the case of the Hurricanes, the problem was resolved by selecting the Republic Thunderbolt. Initially, the RAF was ready to buy some of these fighters, though numbers were expected to be low. This was not how it turned out.

The RAF's reluctance regarding the Thunderbolt stemmed from the first tests it conducted on the type. In 1942, along with many other American aircraft, the RAF had tested the P-47B. This variant was known to have a lot of shortcomings and was never used on operations. Even then, if the RAF had wanted to introduce the Thunderbolt into its inventory, the number of aircraft the US Government was ready to release was so small that it would have been totally impracticable to do so. By 1943, though, the P-47 had been significantly improved and the D-model was in large-scale production. Moreover, the RAF had been witness to the first, and very encouraging, combat operations of the Thunderbolt in Europe. Furthermore, the P-47 was to become the backbone of the 9th Air Force, the USAAF's counterpart to 2 TAF, which was then under formation, where the type proved to be an efficient and effective fighter-bomber.

Thus, the idea was soon accepted that the Thunderbolt would succeed the Hurricane in the Mediterranean. This was a logical step, as the USAAF introduced it as a fighter-bomber in the MTO by the end of 1943. The Thunderbolt was also earmarked as the successor to the Hurricane in the Far East where its excellent long-range capabilities would be of benefit. However, in spring 1944, when the first Thunderbolts were shipped from the USA, the air war in Italy had changed and the Luftwaffe was no longer a major threat. The decision was therefore taken to not replace the Hurricanes with Thunderbolts, and eventually all allocations for combat

A side view of Thunderbolt Mk.II HD267 at Farmingdale (NY) where the type was built. It is a P-47-D-25, the first sub-variant to be equipped with the bubble canopy.

units were reserved for units in the Far East. That said, the RAF still saw the Thunderbolt as an interim fighter-bomber pending the availability of more Mustangs expected in 1945 or 1946 as production was planned to increase considerably by that time. In other words, whatever good service the Thunderbolt could provide in the Far East did not matter as the countdown to its replacement had already started when the first aircraft reached India. It was scheduled to be withdrawn from use by the end of 1946.

DETAILING THE MARK

The RAF used the only model available to foreign operators, the D. Not all D-models were the same, however, as there were a lot of major differences introduced between the first and last production blocks. The RAF took charge of its Thunderbolts as a new block was put into production. Hence the RAF took charge of eight blocks, five designated the Mk.II. The first three blocks became the Thunderbolt Mk.I (see '*SQUADRONS! No. 2*'). The five Thunderbolt Mk.II blocks were:

<u>P-47D-25-RE</u>: Introduced the Plexiglass bubble canopy and a totally new appearance. While the Americans kept the basic denomination of P-47D (even though the denomination of P-47L was at first retained), for the British this change was enough to justify a new mark. Otherwise, there were only slight differences to a P-47D-22-RE (the last Thunderbolt Mk.I batch), such as the internal fuel capacity increased by 370 US gallons and, in the rear fuselage, the addition of two oxygen bottles. The RAF took charge of ninety of them (**HD182-HD271**) between May and June 1944, formerly 42-26477 to 26506, 42-26593 to 26622 and 42-26722 to 26751.

<u>P-47D-27-RE</u>: Only thirty of this block were supplied (**HD272-HD301**), formerly 42-26885 to 26914. They were similar to the D-25-RE, but the engine was capable of an extra 130 horsepower, in case of emergency, by water injection, had a new starter and the drop tanks were improved. These aircraft were delivered between June and August 1944.

<u>P-47D-28-RE</u>: Similar to the D-27-RE, the D-28-RE differed by being equipped with a Curtiss Electric C542S 'paddleblade' propeller and included several minor changes. One hundred and seventy were taken on RAF charge (**KJ128-KJ297**). The deliveries took place between July and November 1944. Formerly 44-19619 to 19658, 44-19806 to 19845, 44-19967 to 20006, 44-20158 to 20197, and 44-20298 to 20307.

<u>P-47D-30-RE & 30-RA</u>: The P-47D-30 was the largest production run of any variant of Thunderbolts and, consequently, as with the USAAF, the D-30-RE and RA (the latter being built at Evansville, Indiana, while the others were built at Farmingdale, New York) became the major sub-types used by the RAF, 295 in all (**KJ298-KJ367, KL168-KL347, KL842-KL886**), formerly 44-20308 to 20337, 44-20488 to 20527, 44-20628 to 20657, 44-20738 to 20797, 44-20817 to 20846, 44-20877 to 20906, 44-20947 to 20976 and 44-90076 to 90120. Of these, four (KL210, KL276, KL322 and KL325) were not delivered to the RAF, having been damaged at various stages of the process, and were eventually repossessed by the USAAF and replaced by four late production D-

A side view of KJ299, one of the first two D-30 sub-types built for the RAF. As a new sub-type, it was sent, along with KJ298, to the UK for various evaluations. The first batches of Thunderbolts were camouflaged. However, having no RAF paint in stock, for Thunderbolts or any of the other US types delivered to the RAF, British colours were substituted by American equivalents - Olive Drab and Sea Grey on top, and Light Grey for the undersurfaces.

Thunderbolt II KJ298 seen in open storage at No. 51 MU in the UK and awaiting the scrapman. It was finally struck off charge on 12 March 1947.

30-RE aircraft (**KL838-KL841**), 44-21046, 21049, 21047 and 21048. Delivered between October 1944 and June 1945. From KL288 onwards, the Thunderbolt Mk IIs were delivered unpainted.

<u>P-47D-40-RA</u>: The last variant built, the P-47D-40-RA introduced a small dorsal fin fillet in front of the vertical tail to eliminate the flutter problem (sometimes retrofitted to previous variants) and had provision for zero-point rocket pylons on the underside of the wing in place of the old bazooka tube launchers of the earlier versions. Ninety of these were allocated to the British (**KL887-KL976**), but only the first one (44-90335) was taken on charge by the RAF. The others were cancelled due to the surplus of Thunderbolts the RAF had on charge by mid-1945, numbers well over what was needed to cover the squadrons selected to participate in the liberation of Malaya and Singapore, and also because the long awaited Mustangs had already begun to be shipped to India at the time (see '*SQUADRONS! No. 11*'). Spitfire Mk.XIVs and Tempest Mk.IIs were also expected to arrive by the end of the year.

These five blocks constituted the RAF's Thunderbolt Mk.II deliveries, of which 675 were ordered and 586 delivered between 15 May 1944 and 28 June 1945. In all, the RAF took delivery of 825 Thunderbolts, becoming the second largest user of the type after the USAAF.

GENERAL USE OF THE THUNDERBOLTS BY THE RAF
While all Thunderbolts were reserved for Far East squadrons, a handful were shipped to the UK for testing. Thus, four Thunderbolt Mk.IIs, representing almost one of each US block (HD182, KJ298, KJ299 and KL887), found their way to the UK, with all but KL887 being test flown by the A&AEE and various test units in 1944 and 1945. HD182, the first Mk.II, arrived soon after the Mk.Is, in May 1944, and was used to conduct various tests until it was struck off charge on 13 December 1946. It was joined by KJ298 and KJ299 in November 1944. These aircraft lasted until the end of 1945 (KJ299) and April 1946 (KJ298) before they were sold for scrap one year later. When the Thunderbolts needed to be modified for testing, Heston Aircraft was contracted to carry out the work. For KL887, however, the only D-40, while it reached England, it arrived too late to be test flown and was left unused at No.51 MU from June 1945 until being sold for scrap in 1947. Therefore, 821 Thunderbolts were available for operational and training units outside the UK.

In January 1944, the front line units in India Command/ACSEA comprised twelve Hurricane squadrons mainly employed as fighter-bomber units. There was a scheduled allocation of sixty Thunderbolts per month between January and June 1944, then eighty aircraft per month for the three following months. Taking wastage in training into account, the RAF planned to convert eight 16-aircraft squadrons to Thunderbolts during the monsoon season when air activity tended to be negligible. The remaining allocations from October 1944 onwards would serve to maintain the operational squadrons. This was the case because the attrition rate was expected to be high regardless of combat losses as the tough climate and terrain hampered servicing at squadron level. While repairs and aircraft salvage were possible in Europe, it was exceptionally difficult in Burma/India and many repairable aircraft were reduced to components due to a lack of the right facilities. This was useful in any event, as the Thunderbolt units faced a recurrent shortage of spare parts. Nevertheless, many aircraft were abandoned as it was uneconomical and hazardous for a salvage team to attempt a recovery.

At first, and to make things easier for the maintenance personnel, while training could have been carried out on both types at the same time, the squadrons were selected for either the Thunderbolt Mk.I or the Mk.II. However, some of the first examples to arrive in India suffered from exposure to seawater during shipment and had to be cleaned up after being uncrated. This took time.

Nevertheless, some were so damaged they were never cleaned and were written off after inspection. This damage seems to have occurred to the first few Mk.Is only and subsequent batches received much more attention and protection. For the Mk.II, only four are known to have been written off upon arrival in India - KJ352, KL241, KL319 and KL340 - either because of corrosion or damage sustained during the crossing. Thus, plans had to be changed and the first squadrons became operational with whatever was available. Many had to go to war with a mix of Thunderbolt Mk.Is and Mk.IIs, with the number of each varying from one squadron to another. Despite this, the attrition rate remained lower than expected and at the end of May, after the liberation of Rangoon, the RAF had 631 Thunderbolts on hand (including 458 Mk.IIs). More than 500 or so were available for Far East operations and the possibility of converting three further Hurricane squadrons in spring 1945 became a reality. At the same time, the Thunderbolt Mk.I was withdrawn from front-line units and by July 1945 all Thunderbolt units were flying the Mk.II. About 450 examples of the Mk.II were available in India, but this number decreased rapidly with the disbandment of the Thunderbolt units and, in May 1946, while all surviving Thunderbolts held in Egypt had been struck off charge, the RAF maintained 65 aircraft for the last two units still operating the type in the Netherlands East Indies (Nos. 60 and 81 Squadrons). This was reduced to fifty in July 1946 as only one squadron was still flying the Thunderbolt. Fifty aircraft was enough to maintain the necessary operational level for 60 Squadron, but its time for new aircraft soon came and the surviving Thunderbolts were soon struck off charge. None remained to see in the New Year of 1947.

Generally speaking the 'T-Bolt' had a big advantage by having a radial, air-cooled engine that did not have the major challenges of operating liquid-cooled engines in hot climates. It also had the long range that the Spitfire and Hurricane lacked. In the OTUs, the type was often chosen for these reasons, and the Spitfire didn't automatically win the pilots' favour. In a dogfight, the Thunderbolt was generally inferior to the Spitfire. As was sometimes said after training: "Evasive action in a T-Bolt is taken by undoing straps and running round the cockpit"! In the Far East, Japanese fighters were no longer a major threat when the Thunderbolt was introduced into service. In the tough combat conditions of the Far East, the pilots who had converted to the type were quick to appreciate its qualities. Few had cause to regret the choice, and most liked the aircraft and were confident in its reliability and toughness. The pilots had a real preference for the Mk.II because of its bubble canopy, and were generally glad to give up the Mk.I.

From a tactical point of view, the RAF, within 3 TAF, had split its units into two Groups (Nos. 224 and 221) for the two main land operations: Arakan and the Central (Imphal) Front respectively. The RAF re-organised and renamed its Wings on 1 October 1944, just after the Thunderbolt began operational flying, and by the end of 1944 three wings were operating Thunderbolts, sometimes alongside other types, mainly Hurricanes (Nos. 904, 905 and 910 Wings). The Thunderbolt squadrons moved from one Wing to another in response to local tactical needs. Unlike the Mk.I, which participated in only a single major campaign, the recapture of Burma, which started in December 1944, the Mk.II was used continuously from the first operational days of the type in the Far East to VJ-Day and even beyond as the Thunderbolt was selected to help the Dutch restore their sovereignty over the NEI (part of No. 910 Wing). By the summer of 1945, all Thunderbolt units were flying the newer aircraft and, in all, 13,500 sorties were flown by the Mk.II (including 11,800 against the Japanese) compared to 5000 sorties flown by the Mk.I. A single half-share air victory was claimed by the Mk.II.

For this issue, the Thunderbolt Mk.II's story will only be told for the following units: 5, 30, 34, 42, 60, 79, 81, 113, 123, 131, 134, 135, 146, 258, 261, 615 and the relevant training units.

A derelict KL887 before it was scrapped in March 1947. KL887 was the last Thunderbolt taken on RAF charge. All subsequent aircraft were cancelled.

On 30 June, the RAF in the Far East has re-orginised the wings in preparation of Operation 'Ziper'. Some positions were still to be filled in, being generaly vacant. Note that if the Wing leader had made their career as a fighter pilot, the Officer Commandings would all coming from the Bomber Command by the end of July.

No. 904 Wing
OC: G/C George F. Chater, replaced by G/C David J.P. Lee from the 6th
Wing Leader: W/C Sydney A.H. Whitehouse (not yet arrived, effective the 21st)

No. 60 Squadron
No. 131 Squadron
No. 258 Squadron
No. 261 Squadron

No. 905 Wing
OC: G/C Raymond W.P. Collings (not yet arrived, effective the 23rd)
Wing Leader: W/C Evan O. Richmond-Watson

No. 5 Squadron
No. 30 Squadron
No. 81 Squadron

No. 910 Wing
OC: G/C Gordon C.O. Key
Wing Leader: W/C John I. Kilmartin (not yet arrived, effective the 21st)

No. 34 Squadron
No. 42 Squadron
No. 79 Squadron
No. 113 Squadron

By the middle of summer 1945, the three wing commander flying positions were intended for three veterans of the Battle of Britain. From left to right: Wing Commanders Sydney A.H. Whitehouse, Evan O. Richmond-Watson and John I. Kilmartin. Kilmartin was a newcomer in the Far East, but Whitehouse and Richmond-Watson served there from 1943. Evan Watson, as he was known at the time, led 136 Sqn between March and October. That year, however, Watson changed his name to Richmond-Watson. Interestingly, the OC positions were occupied by former bomber pilots. *(Richmond-Watson family middle)*

Victories - confirmed or probable claims: 1.0

First operational sortie:
16.10.44
Last operational sortie:
13.05.45

Number of sorties: ca. 1,450

Total aircraft written-off: 21

Aircraft lost on operations: 8
Aircraft lost in accidents: 13

Squadron code letters:
RS

COMMANDING OFFICERS

S/L Thomas A. Stevens	RAF No. 86669	RAF	...	24.05.45
F/L Harry F. Whidborne (TEMP.)	RAF No. 117703	RAF	24.05.45	29.07.45
S/L Thomas H. Meyer	RAF No. 114915	RAF	29.07.45	...

SQUADRON USAGE

Having started the war on Blenheims fitted with gun packs, No. 30 Squadron became a single-engine fighter unit in May 1941 when it re-equipped with Hurricanes. In the summer of 1944, it was selected to convert on the Thunderbolt. By October , the squadron had completed its training and began operations with the Thunderbolt Mk.I from Chittagong in India. A handful of Mk.IIs was also on hand, but these were generally flown by the flight commanders and the CO (HD192, HD208, HD267 and HD289/RS-S). During that phase, one Thunderbolt Mk.II, HD267, was badly damaged when it caught fire on start up. Nobody was hurt but was aircraft was struck off charge on 5 October after investigations. The squadron mounted its first operation on 16 October when two Thunderbolts, one of each mark, were detailed to attack bashas during a 'Rhubarb'. The Mk.II was flown by F/L E. Holmgren (RCAF). The squadron flew 36 sorties in October, mainly with Mk.Is, but on 31 October it lost one of the newly arrived Mk.IIs (HD264) during training when Sgt Waters failed to get clear on take-off and crashed 200 yards off the end of the runway. The aircraft burst into flames and Waters was killed instantly. At the end of October, the squadron received more Mk.IIs which were to replace the Mk.I by the end of the month. These Thunderbolts were HD191, HD204, HD243, HD245, HD258, HD265/RS-G, HD272, HD280/RS-K, HD289/RS-S, HD294, HD298/RS-U, HD299/RS-J and KJ131/RS-Y were added to the inventory. The withdrawal was slowed down due to the loss of some Mk.IIs. This forced the squadron to keep some Mk.Is operational. On 3 November, the unit joined the Thunderbolts of No. 135 Squadron for a sweep over Mingaladon airfield. Two of 30's aircraft were obliged to return early due to technical problems and W/O H.C. Edwards (RNZAF) was seen to crash in enemy territory after his engine caught fire. He was captured, but survived the harsh Japanese treatment meted out to prisoners. The next day, the squadron was called to escort Liberators to their target, the Insein railway workshops at Rangoon. The fighters arrived at the meeting point early and, after a wide sweep

Flight Lieutenant Harry Whidborne was the only Commonwealth pilot to make a full claim on a Thunderbolt Mk.II. He was awarded the DFC at the end of the war. *(via JF Hamlin)*

out to sea, arrived too late so that only Red Section in the lead and the USAAF P-38s of the 459th Fighter Squadron found the Libs, while the rest returned to Cox's Bazar which was sometimes used by squadron detachments. As the Liberators turned away from the target after dropping their bombs, two enemy aircraft identified as Ki-44 'Tojos' appeared at 12,000 feet and made an attack on the trailing bombers. One made a pass and pulled up to the right and the other made a pass and dived away. Red Leader, F/L Whidmore, in HD289, attacked the one that pulled up and observed strikes in the cockpit area that caused the enemy aircraft to catch fire and turn nose down, giving the opportunity for a second burst at very close range. Flight Lieutenant T.H. Fulford also obtained a wide angle shot on the same aircraft and saw smoke trailing from it. The Japanese spiralled down and was seen to crash into the ground for a victory that would later be confirmed by pilots of the 459th FS. The next few days saw the squadron continue to provide escorts to various aircraft, including Dakotas involved in supply sorties. On the 9th, the unit flew various patrols and escorts for Dakotas and it was while returning from one such op that P/O E.A. McKenzie (RAAF) made a heavy landing that badly damaged his aircraft. After investigating the damage, the decision was made to not repair the aircraft and it was subsequently converted to components. To replace recent losses, Thunderbolts HD205 and KJ150 were taken on charge. On 17 November, twelve Thunderbolts carried out a fighter sweep over the airfields around Rangoon. They climbed to 23,000 feet in battle formation with 135 Squadron slightly above. On approaching the target area they descended to 19,000 feet. No enemy was seen at Pabst, Zayatkwin or Hmawbi, but things were different between there and Mingaladon when about twelve Japanese fighters were seen to be adopting defensive orbiting patterns between 8000 and 10,000 feet. All of the Thunderbolts dropped their extra fuel tanks and Red Section was the first to dive to attack. The engagement lasted ten minutes, but no claims were made. Blue Section followed about a thousand yards behind and made a concentrated attack on three aircraft at 8000 feet, but here too no claim was made. The other aircraft of the squadron did not engage. Alongside the frustration of not having made a single claim, the T-Bolts faced various technical problems: three could not fully detach their long-range tanks, two others had oil on their windscreens, and another two suffered persistent engine trouble. All were lucky to return home despite some being diverted to other airfields. Trouble continued as, on landing at Chittagong, two Thunderbolts, HD294 and HD298, collided. Flying Officer V.B.J. Carson (RCAF) escaped major injury, but W/O I.G. Hardy, a New Zealander serving in the RAAF was badly injured and died from his injuries soon after. Two days later the squadron provided escort, with 135 Squadron, as top cover for 22 Liberators bombing railways at Mokpalin. The various sections were spread out between 11,000 feet and 14,000 feet when, at about ten miles from the target, White Section, flying at 14,000 feet, was jumped in quick succession by 'Oscars' approaching from the north. At the first attack, White Section jettisoned tanks and broke away to the left to 12,000 feet to avoid the four Japanese fighters. They were jumped again by three more 'Oscars' forcing three of the Thunderbolts to come down to 6000 feet, losing sight of the bombers in the process. At the same time, Blue Leader, F/L H.F. Whidborne, flying at 13,000 feet, made a pass at an 'Oscar', but failed to damage it. Seven of 30 Squadron's aircraft continued to escort the bombers to the target and the rest of the operation was flown without any incident, except that F/Sgt H.H. Martin overshot the runway in HD205 and damaged the fighter enough for it to be beyond economical repair and eventually converted to spare parts. The last op of the month took place on the 23rd, and was another escort of Libs, but American ones this time. It was uneventful. In all 120 sorties were flown in November, with all but nine of them on the Mk.II. To make up for attrition, the squadron took charge of new Thunderbolts - HD248, HD269/RS-S, KJ128, KJ140/RS-B, KJ146, KJ155 and KJ187 - in the last week of November.

With nice weather in December, the squadron almost doubled its number of sorties from the month before. The aircraft moved to

Thunderbolt HD265/RS-G was among the first Mk.IIs to become operational with 30 Sqn at the end of October 1944. HD265 is ready for an escort sortie with a 137 US gallon fuel tank under each wing.

Some of 30 Squadron's pilots during their conversion course at Yelahanka during the summer of 1944. Back row: W/O N.G. Mills, F/O M.J. Kidd (RAAF), F/L E.F. Holmgren (RCAF), F/O G.C. Boyer, F/L T.H. Fulford, P/O P.M. Hamilton, and F/Sgt J.P. Pyman. Front row: W/O D.R. Blair, P/O G.G. Newell (†14.08.44), W/O K.J. Knodler (RAAF - †14.08.44), W/O C.R. Wright (RCAF), and F/L H.F. Whidborne. *(via JF Hamlin)*

Jumchar on 10 December, but a new role was also assigned. The squadron was now to fly fighter-bomber ops, the majority in support of the 25th Indian Division and the 81st West African Division. In all, 205 sorties were flown in December. This new role was also occasionally complemented by escorts or patrols. On 16 December, Thunderbolt KJ187 crashed on take-off for a close-support sortie and the aircraft, after partial disintegration, came to rest on its back and caught fire. The pilot, W/O 'Curly' Lacasse (RCAF) was extracted after a hole was dug underneath the cockpit. He was transferred to hospital with burns to his face, hands and legs. Another mishap occurred two weeks later when the CO suffered a very unpleasant experience when the engine of his Thunderbolt, the recently arrived KJ132, cut in the circuit while returning from a ground support sortie. He made a forced-landing in a paddy 500 yards from the airfield and was fortunate to escape unscathed. Heavy rains early in January quickly rendered the airfield useless and that had an impact on operational activity. Despite this, no less than 320 sorties were carried out that month.

By the end of January, the squadron was now flying the Thunderbolt Mk.II (D-28), fitted with the Curtiss 'paddleblade' propeller, much to the satisfaction of the pilots. Thunderbolts HD193/RS-H, KJ149/RS-I, KJ157, KJ213, KJ220, KJ223, KJ240/RS-W, KJ258, KJ271 and KJ276 were put into service, but KJ157 only had a short career with the squadron as it collided with HD280 while taxiing to the parking area on return from a bombing op on 22 January. No casualties was reported, but KJ157 was too damaged to be repaired and would find a second life as a spare parts source for other Thunderbolts. Strafing sorties continued throughout the month and, altogether, more than 360 500-lb bombs were dropped and 72,500 rounds of 0.50-in ammunition fired. Also, by the end of the month, the unit had begun to drop its first Napalm tanks, a new weapon that had recently been added in the Allies' inventory.

A few showers in February were enough to render the airfield at Chittagong unserviceable for almost half the month. Therefore, the squadron had to mainly operate from Cox's Bazar to support XV Corps advancing on the Arakan front. This support consisted of 192,000-lb of bombs, 11,748 gallons of Napalm and 185,000 rounds of 0.50-in. The targets remained the same: enemy guns, bunkers, defensive positions, troop concentrations, stores, dumps, bridges and roads, to name a few. Sometimes, the squadron was requested to fly some defensive or counter battery patrols over newly won bridgeheads. Two escorts for American Liberators were also flown, the first on the 11th and the second on the 28th. In all, about 325 sorties were recorded in February. That would be the highest number of sorties flown by the squadron on Thunderbolts. This was helped by good serviceability of the aircraft despite the recurring problem of spare parts supply for both engine and airframe components. Also, only one Thunderbolt was written-off in February. This occurred on the 24th when twelve aircraft flew to Cox's Bazar to be fitted with Napalm tanks for two operations later that day. On landing, KJ128, flown by Sgt B.A.T. Rattenbury, burst a tyre, swung off the runway and overturned on sandy soil. Sadly, Rattenbury was found to be dead. In February, Thunderbolts KJ264, KJ267, KJ275 and KJ281/RS-R were included in the squadron's inventory to balance the withdrawal of some earlier aircraft sent for overhaul.

In March, operational activity was limited to 270 sorties (representing 800 hours of flight). The reduction was not because of the weather, which was fine during the month, but simply because, after the 14th, the squadron was unable to provide immediate close support to XV Corps, as the advance into the enemy lines stretched the fighter bombers' endurance. That didn't mean that the unit

One hundred thirty-seven gallon long-range drop tanks amassed next to the Republic Thunderbolt Mk.IIs of 30 Sqn as they are readied for a sortie at Cox's Bazar in the autumn of 1944. Thunderbolts RS-C and RS-G (HD265) can be seen in this photo.

The last wartime CO was S/L Thomas 'Tim' Meyer who had previously commanded 615 Sqn on Spitfires between September 1944 and June 1945. He had also previously served with 155 Sqn flying Mohawks and Spitfires. *(A. Thomas)*

became inactive as it was usually called once a day to carry out ground attacks behind the front. Pilots had to fly with long-range drop tanks, limiting their weapons load, and most of the time the 90-gallon tanks had issues. To continue to provide efficient ground support, the squadron moved south to Akyab on 24 April and because of this the squadron was able to fly 120 sorties in a short time. No operations were flown after the 12th as the squadron stood down ahead of the move. The first sortie from Akyab was carried out on the 29th. In April, the unit received its first D-30 models in the form of KL183/RS-S and KL216. In May, with the launch of Operation *Dracula*, the liberation of Rangoon that ended on 13 May, the squadron provided close to 100 sorties in support of ground forces. On 18 May, the squadron made another move to Chakulia. Shortly after the end of operations, fortunately for the RAF, a severe storm with winds in excess of 100 mph caused great havoc at Chakulia and, although the aircraft were picketed, three Thunderbolts were damaged beyond repair (KJ140, KJ191, KJ240) while others were damaged, but repairable. Three days later, another storm caused a lot of damage and sealed the fate of another Thunderbolt (KJ267). Between those two days, the CO left for Bombay on his way to the UK. Stevens would never return to the unit as he was posted to a HQ position with 224 Group. However these events had some consequences in June and reduced the air activity as the mechanics spent most of their time repairing the storm-tossed Thunderbolts. Only 37 hours of non-operational flights were performed in June during which one Thunderbolt, KJ193, was badly damaged in an accident when the pilot, F/O E.A. McKenzie, was taken ill and had to make a forced-landing during a liaison flight. He broke a leg and suffered various cuts, but was otherwise safe. In July, the squadron moved to Vizagapatam and, upon arrival, training was resumed with all but two of the 23.15 hours of flight being performed by Thunderbolts. However, the situation was not ideal for the squadron, which was slow to recover to its full strength of aircraft, still without any official CO to replace Stevens, and, regarding pilots, facing a shortage with many of the long-serving men being tour expired, or close to it, and the announcement of the withdrawal of Dominion personnel from SEA Command. Soon the squadron was reduced to half its regular strength. So, the fact that the squadron flew 268.2 hours in July was quite an accomplishment. To make things worse, one Thunderbolt was wrecked on the 24th (KJ149) when F/L Jutsum hit a bund at the end of the runway while taking-off for a practice flight with F/L A.D. Dick. The impact sheared the port oleo completely, while the other leg of the undercarriage would not retract fully, one flap was damaged, and the gun panel on the starboard wing burst open. After having considered a belly landing, it was decided that bailing out was the best option. The aircraft was abandoned along the coast about eight miles south of the airfield. Slightly injured, the pilot was later recovered safe. The new CO, S/L 'Tim' Meyer, finally arrived on the 29th. Meyer took over the squadron the same day, having arrived from 615 Squadron which he had led since the previous September. Training continued in August and, unfortunately, one pilot was killed on 12 August in KL222/RS-W during the take-off for bombing practice. Pilot Officer F.G. Kent was seen to crash two miles south west of the airfield. Five days later, Thunderbolt KJ271 was also lost in an accident when the engine gave trouble on take-off and the pilot decided to throttle back. The aircraft eventually ran into soft sand at the end of the runway and, ultimately, would not be repaired owing to the end of war. In all, 366 hours over 309 flights were flown that month. The squadron would continue to fly the Thunderbolt until March 1946 after a considered move to the NEI was cancelled. In the last month of operation, two Thunderbolts were wrecked within two days. The first was KL343 on 22 March when the pilot, Flying Officer F.C. Summer, detected the presence of hydraulic fluid leaking into the cockpit. As there were clear indications of more serious problems, he decided to land as a precaution, but since there was no airfield nearby he made a belly landing in an open field. The next day, it was the turn of KL287 which suffered an engine failure on approach to Bhopal and ended up on its back. The pilot, Sgt W.E. Tatlow, escaped serious injury. The Thunderbolts were replaced by a British-made aircraft, the Tempest Mk. II, soon after.

Claims - 30 Squadron (Confirmed and Probable)

Date	Pilot	SN	Origin	Type	Serial	Code	Nb	Cat.
03.11.44	F/L Harry F. **WHIDBORNE**	RAF No. 117703	RAF	Ki-44	**HD289**	RS-S	1.0	C
					Total: 1.0			

During the summer of 1945, when based at Vizagapatam, 30 Sqn received brand new, unpainted Thunderbolts, like KL308/RS-C, but also some of the latest from the P-47D-30-RA batch, like KL881/RS-H and KL855/RS-J. *(via J.F. Hamlin)*

Thunderbolt HD298/RS-U about to touch down after an uneventful escort as can be seen by the still attached long-range fuel tanks. The aircraft would be lost soon after, on 17 November, in a collision that cost the life of its pilot.

Summary of the aircraft lost on Operations - 30 Squadron

Date	Pilot	S/N	Origin	Serial	Code	Fate
03.11.44	W/O Howard C. **Edwards**	NZ413171	RNZAF	**HD245**		**PoW**
09.11.44	P/O Ernest A. **McKenzie**	Aus. 420772	RAAF	**HD289**	RS-S	-
17.11.44	F/O Vernon B.J. **Carson**	Can./ J.23447	RCAF	**HD294**		-
	W/O Ian G. **Hardy**	Aus. 420880	(NZ)/RAAF	**HD298**	RS-U	†
19.11.44	F/Sgt Harold H. **Martin**	RAF No. 1495453	RAF	**HD205**		-
16.12.44	W/O Edward M. **LaCasse**	Can./ R. 67136	RCAF	**KJ187**		-
30.12.44	S/L Thomas A. **Stevens**	RAF No. 86669	RAF	**KJ132**		-
22.01.45	W/O John D. **Knowles**	RAF No. 1384416	RAF	**KJ157**		-

Total: 8

Date	Pilot	S/N	Origin	Serial	Code	Fate
22.09.44	*Caught fire starting up*	-	-	**HD267**		-
31.10.44	Sgt Victor A. **WATERS**	RAF No. 1605509	RAF	**HD264**		†
24.02.45	Sgt Bernard A. T. **RATTENBURY**	RAF No. 1804463	RAF	**KJ128**	RS-X	†
23.05.45	*Destroyed in gale*	-	-	**KJ140**	RS-B	-
	Destroyed in gale	-	-	**KJ191**	RS-C	-
	Destroyed in gale	-	-	**KJ240**	RS-W	-
26.05.45	*Destroyed in gale*	-	-	**KJ267**		-
30.06.45	F/O Ernest A. **MCKENZIE**	AUS. 420772	RAAF	**KJ193**	RS-H	-
24.07.45	F/L Alan D. **DICK**	RAF No. 141539	RAF	**KJ149**	RS-I	-
12.08.45	P/O Frederick G. **KENT**	RAF No. 181419	RAF	**KL222**	RS-W	†
19.08.45	F/Sgt Rowland G. **SIMPSON**	RAF No. 1583845	RAF	**KJ271**		-
22.03.46	F/O Frank C. **SUMNER**	RAF No. 195209	RAF	**KL343**		-
23.03.46	F/Sgt William H. **TATLOW**	RAF No. 1685540	RAF	**KL287**		-

Total: 13

Thunderbolt KJ140 seen in the autumn of 1944. It was damaged beyond repair during a gale in May 1945. Note the squadron's palm tree badge painted on the white fin band.

Victories - confirmed or probable claims: 0.5

First operational sortie:
07.12.44

Last operational sortie:
14.05.45

Number of sorties: ca. 1,250

Total aircraft written-off: 8

Aircraft lost on operations: 2
Aircraft lost in accidents: 6

Squadron code letters:
ZT

COMMANDING OFFICERS

S/L Neil CAMERON	RAF No. 102585	RAF	...	01.08.45
S/L William B. BERRY	RAF No. 45593	RAF	01.08.45	05.12.45
F/L Denis M. FINN	RAF No. 133445	RAF	05.12.45	...

SQUADRON USAGE

No. 258 Squadron had already led a chaotic existence when it began its conversion to the Thunderbolt at the end of the summer of 1944. Sent to Singapore with its Hurricanes in early 1942, it became one of the victims of the disaster that occurred with the fall of Singapore. It was re-formed in Ceylon soon afterwards and was sent to India in 1943 where it served as a fighter-bomber unit. By the summer of 1944, it was ready to relinquish its ageing Hurricanes and was selected to fly Thunderbolts. The last flight by a squadron Hurricane took place on 5 August. At the time, the unit was led by S/L Neil Cameron and based at Yelahanka. Ground school on the Thunderbolt began over the next few days under the supervision of No. 1670 CU. The first seven Thunderbolt Mk.Is arrived on 8 September, ferried by pilots of No. 134 Squadron, with six more delivered on the 10th, and the last three (Mk.IIs) arriving on the 13th. The training program was accelerated and by the end of September over 450 hours had been flown, but not without losses, however, as, during a formation flight, two Mk.Is collided at 500 feet (see 'SQUADRONS! No. 2'). In October 500 more hours were flown without any incidents to report. On 2 November, the squadron lost another two Thunderbolt Mk.Is, both during a practice interception. These aircraft were replaced by Mk.IIs, complicating the maintenance of the squadron fleet with eleven Mk.Is and five Mk.IIs on hand. However, the Mk.Is saw the majority of use during the month, completing 230 hours while the Mk.IIs only flew 80. On 11 October, while performing aerobatics between 30,000 and 37,000 feet, the Thunderbolt (HD198) of F/O C.C. Betts (RAAF) entered an inverted flat spin. Betts was unable to recover and evacuated the aircraft safely at 4500 feet.

Neil Cameron was given command of 258 Sqn in February 1944 when it was equipped with Hurricanes. He would continue to lead the squadron until the end of the war and oversaw all of the squadron's Thunderbolt flying. He was made Companion of the DSO in October for his leadership, remained with the RAF after the war and reached the rank of Marshal of the RAF in 1977 before retiring in 1979. *(A. Thomas)*

Thunderbolt HD244/ZT-Z under maintenance. Issued to 258 Sqn in November, HD244 survived the aerial campaign and was eventually struck off charge on 11 April 1946. *(A. Thomas)*

Training completed, 258 moved to Ratnap in Burma at the end of November, to begin operations against the Japanese, with the same mix of Thunderbolts. The Mk.IIs - HD217/V, HD236/W, HD244/Z, HD259 and HD292/L - were gathered together in B Flight. It had been decided to send the squadron into combat with Mk.IIs, but, due to a lack of available Mk.IIs, this objective could not be met, forcing the pilots to start ops on both marks. The first sorties were flown on 7 December with seven Mk.Is and the five Mk.IIs flying together for a fighter sweep in the morning (led by S/L Cameron in HD292). The squadron was part of 905 Wing at the time. The situation regarding equipment improved during the month and the Mk.Is were gradually replaced by Mk.IIs. By the end of the month, there were nine Mk.Is on strength. Replacement aircraft continued to arrive in January and eventually the unit was totally re-equipped with the Mk.II by mid-January. This had also been expedited by exchanging the remaining Mk.Is with the Mk.IIs No. 5 Squadron had on charge. The Mk.IIs on hand at the time were HD185, HD196/J, HD217/V, HD222, HD227, HD236/W, HD244/Z, HD256, HD279, HD288, HD290, HD292/L, KJ130/D, KJ138, KJ165/A, KJ229 and KJ314/J, for a full complement of sixteen Thunderbolts. The last sorties on Mk.Is were recorded on the 18th. In December 1944 and January 1945, the squadron was involved in close ground support and participated in the invasions of Akyab Island, from 3 January onwards, and Ramree Island, from the 21st, with detachments at Cox's Bazar. In January, 258 flew 350 sorties (all but forty on the Mk.II) and dropped 572 500-lb bombs, 22 90-gallon Napalm tanks and expended 167,170 rounds of ammunition. In the first days of February, the squadron continued its ground support missions, mainly for 25th Indian Division, and sustained its first loss on operations when F/O F.T. Kelf (RAAF) suffered an engine failure as he left the target early in the morning of the 2nd during the first op of the day. He made a perfect wheels-up landing in a field and was picked up by a Stinson L-5 and returned to the squadron after having been entertained by the Army. Eight days later on the 10th, the squadron sustained another loss when moving to Cox's Bazar. P/O D.W.B Lansdown crashed on take-off and was killed while proceeding to the advance field for a further operation the next day. The next day on the 11th, taking-off from Cox's Bazar, the squadron was tasked with escorting 84 B-24 Liberators from the 7th BG and 99, 215, 355 and 356 Squadrons. They were joined by 59 B-29 Superfortresses from XX Bomber Command. The escort was also made up of Thunderbolts from Nos. 30 and 134 Squadrons and P-38s from the 459th Fighter Squadron of the USAAF. Over the target, six Ki-61 'Tony' fighters rose to intercept and soon the bombers reported being under attack by three of those. The escort wasn't inactive and S/L Cameron made an approach on the same aircraft sighted by the gunners of 215 Squadron and, when the second Japanese aircraft went into a dive, Cameron fired a burst of three seconds with 70° deflection from 400 yards. He lost sight of the enemy for a few seconds, but then regained his target and was able to see the pilot bailing out. As the gunners of the 215 Squadron Libs had already fired at this 'Tony' and had claimed it as hit, the 'Tony' was eventually shared between them and Cameron. The crews of 99 Squadron also claimed one Ki-43 destroyed and one more probably destroyed. Over the next few days, and until the end of the month, 258 returned to its ground support task to complete 260 sorties for the month. The number of sorties increased in March with over 325 recorded in support of the 14th Army advancing towards Mandalay. That represented more than 1000 flying hours for the squadron, 147,875 rounds of ammunition fired and 469 bombs dropped. On 22 March, the CO took the squadron to Sadaung for close support of the Army, but the ferry flight ended badly for F/L H.W Seton (RCAF) and P/O R.D. King when King's aircraft (KJ197) hit Seton's (KJ199) on landing. Both pilots escaped injury, but the same could not be said for KJ199 as it caught fire. KJ197 was later repaired. Therefore, only nine Thunderbolts could participate in the op, an uneventful attack on two villages. Despite the losses, the squadron was able to maintain an average of thirteen aircraft available per day. This was a good result considering that the other Thunderbolt squadrons were not as lucky or effective. In April 258 saw its operational activity cut by almost two-thirds with just over 110 sorties flown. From the squadron perspective, nothing noteworthy was achieved. It participated in the liberation of Rangoon in May and would be airborne supporting the Army until the 14th when the monsoon made its annual appearance. The squadron had moved to Kyaukpyu for this task. In May 128 sorties were flown and the month ended with an attack on a concentration of Japanese troops and guns. In all the squadron could be proud of the 1470 combat sorties (including 1250 by Mk.IIs) it flew while equipped with the Thunderbolt. Sadly, one aircraft (HD217) was lost on 7 May when F/L 'Brownie' Brown (RCAF), returning from a sortie with engine trouble, spun in on approach and was killed. By mid-May, the Thunderbolts on strength were HD244/Z, HD292/L, KJ138, KJ213, KJ229, KJ279/H, KJ287, KJ303, KJ304, KJ314/J, KJ336, KJ350, KJ366/X, KL175, KL209, KL240/B and KL324. On 17 May the squadron received instructions to move to Chakulia with 24 hours' notice. Five days later a cyclone passed by causing a lot of damage, including to one Thunderbolt (KJ304) that was later declared beyond economical repair. One week later, a new base, Ulundurpet, south of Madras in India, was allocated to the squadron. It arrived on the 8th and became part of 904 Wing. Air activity remained low in June with only 122 hours flown, including the ferry flight to the new base. In July, a turnover of personnel took place, with Dominion personnel leaving for repatriation and, by the end of June, the squadron had almost become a full RAF unit. Among the pilots who left were the CO who was replaced by S/L W.B. Berry from 1 August. Berry had arrived from No. 4 Squadron IAF which he had led since February. Training for Operation *Zipper* was planned to commence on 16 July, but as most of the aircraft were unserviceable due to a shortage of spare parts, lack of replacement aircraft and non-arrival of maintenance equipment, only four 'T-Bolts' were available daily. Therefore, only 100 hours were flown in July. On 1 August, while on a practice flight, the engine of KL175 cut and its pilot, W/O P.D. Skelt (RNZAF) proceeded to make a forced-landing in a very favourable place where he could save the aircraft or at least get it down with only minor damage. However, when he saw that about 2000 locals were where he wanted to put down, he decided to make his forced-landing in a wood, completely wrecking the aircraft, but luckily escaping any injury. Otherwise, the number of hours flown in August reached 230, but with V-J day announced, Operation *Zipper* was only partially executed. This meant a move to Bobbili, located on the northern coast of the Bay of Bengal, on the 21st. One month later, the squadron could be found in Kuala Lumpur and, including the ferry flights to its new home, just 200 flying hours were completed that month. In October the squadron had to hand over much of its equipment, aircraft and spare parts to Nos. 60 and 81 Squadrons as they departed for Java and, to make things worse, maintenance was undertaken by No. 7131 Service Echelon of 131 Squadron. Consequently, not much flying was done in October, just 25.6 hours! During one of these few flights, on 6 October, KJ361 was seriously damaged while landing with its wheels up on return from an air test. The pilot had failed to lower the undercarriage correctly. The Thunderbolt was a total write-off. In November, things improved a bit with 75 hours flown, but spare parts were still a major problem. On the 17th and 18th, the squadron was called upon to make some low level flights over villages where trouble had arisen between the Malays and Chinese. During those two days, sixteen sorties were flown and dummy attacks carried out over six villages and surrounds in the Seremban and Ipoh areas. Early in December, 7258 Service Echelon finally arrived, but at the same time as the squadrons in Java needed replacement aircraft. Soon eight of the squadron's Thunderbolts had been ferried there. On the 5th, S/L Berry relinquished command to F/L D.M. Finn who had received the DFC while serving with No. 4 Squadron IAF. That month, air activity was very limited, but some demonstration flights were flown. However, with the drawdown of the RAF in the Far East, and considering the chaotic life the squadron had recently led, 258 was not chosen to remain as an operational unit and was disbanded on 31 December.

Thunderbolt KL314/ZT-W in the spring of 1945. It served with 258 Sqn until the summer and later served with 60 Sqn in the NEI. It was lost in the last RAF Thunderbolt accident on 1 October 1946. *(A. Thomas)*

Date	Pilot	SN	Origin	Type	Serial	Code	Nb	Cat.
11.02.45	S/L Neil **CAMERON**	RAF No. 102585	RAF	Ki-61	**HD292**	ZT-L	0.5*	C

*Shared with gunners of No. 215 Squadron

Total: 0.5

Summary of the aircraft lost on Operations - 258 Squadron

Date	Pilot	S/N	Origin	Serial	Code	Fate
02.02.45	F/O Frank T. **KELF**	Aus. 402786	RAAF	**KJ130**	ZT-D	-
07.05.45	F/L Sydney W. **BROWN**	Can./ J.20638	RCAF	**HD217**	ZT-V	†

Total: 2

Summary of the aircraft lost by accident - 258 Squadron

Date	Pilot	S/N	Origin	Serial	Code	Fate
11.10.44	F/O Colin C. **BETTS**	Aus. 402786	RAAF	**HD198**		-
10.02.45	P/O Desmond W.B. **LANSDOWN**	RAF No. 184368	RAF	**KJ185**		†
22.03.45	F/L Hugh W. **SETON**	Can./ J.13483	RCAF	**KJ199**		-
23.05.45	*Destroyed by gale*	-	-	**KJ304**		-
01.08.45	W/O Paul D. **SKELT**	NZ4211669	RNZAF	**KL175**		-
06.10.45	Sgt John L. **EARNSHAW**	RAF No. 1569354	RAF	**KJ361**		-

Total: 6

One of the last Thunderbolt additions was the shiny KL871/ZT-W seen here during the summer of 1945. It became 'W' to replace KL314. Seated in the cockpit is W/O P.D. Skelt, a Kiwi and one of the last remaining Commonwealth pilots of the squadron at the time. *(P.D. Skelt via P. Sortehaug)*

No. 5 Squadron - code OQ

The association of 5 Squadron with the Thunderbolt Mk.II was actually quite brief. Flying the type from October 1944, it went to war with the Mk.I and would be one of the very few squadrons to fly this mark during 1945 (see Squadrons! No. 2). However, the squadron did at first receive some Mk.IIs when it began operations under the command of its New Zealander CO, S/L Cranstone. This caused some trouble for the mechanics with regard to the supply of spare parts, which was already a significant problem for the Thunderbolt as a whole. So, the few Mk.IIs were held in reserve and the few ops flown were usually by the CO who had a preference for HD279. The other known Mk.IIs flying with 5 Squadron by mid-January were HD227 and KJ138. By then, to simplify the situation, an exchange was arranged with No. 258 Squadron, the Mk.IIs being taken on charge by 258 which, in turn, handed over its Mk.Is. Only one Mk.II, KJ208, remained with 5 Squadron and was flown by Cranstone until he left the unit at the end of the month as tour expired.

The squadron continued, therefore, its war with the Mk.I until it ceased operations in May 1945. In June the squadron was based at Vizagapatam on the east coast of India under the command of S/L L.H. Dawes (ex-607 Squadron). On 24 June, with Operation *Zipper* in sight, the squadron moved to Bobbili, a couple of miles north of Vizagapatam, where it finally exchanged its ageing Mk.Is for Mk.IIs. This process took time, however, as it was not until the end of July that a full complement of aircraft was reached. Even so, basic tools were in short supply. At the same time, and as with other units in the Far East, Dominion personnel were replaced by British pilots, most being fresh graduates, in need of further training before becoming operational. Flying resumed, but the shortage of engine oil, hydraulic oil and petrol made this difficult and the Thunderbolts spent little time in the air. This situation was shared with most, if not all, of the units of 221 Group at the time. This, of course, had an impact on morale. Despite this, some flights were carried out, but, as the aircraft could not be maintained as required, some accidents occurred. On 2 August, the undercarriage of KL182 could not be lowered and the pilot, W/O Griffin, who had only three hours on type, had to make a belly landing at Bobbili that sealed the fate of the aircraft. Flights continued on a small scale over the following days, but another Thunderbolt was lost, fortunately without major consequences for the pilot, W/O R. Shanks, when it suffered an engine failure on approach on 10 August (KJ184). This accident occurred when the pilot switched from the main fuel tanks to the auxiliary tanks and the engine was starved of fuel. On the 30th, the squadron left Bobbili for Vizagapatam, and then went to Baigachi near Calcutta on 12 September. However, the war was over for the squadron with the Japanese surrender, but it continued to use its Thunderbolts until February 1946 when Tempest IIs arrived to replace them. Not much flying was done during that period of re-organisation, but one last Thunderbolt was lost in an accident on 20 September when W/O Drake crashed on landing at Baigaichi in KJ256 after having collected the aircraft from Vizagapatam. A brake failure was found to be responsible for the crash. The failure was blamed on a high landing speed, touching down too far along the runway, and subsequent overuse in trying to stop the heavy fighter.

Summary of the aircraft lost by accident - 5 Squadron

Date	Pilot	S/N	Origin	Serial	Code	Fate
02.08.45	W/O Kenneth W. **GRIFFIN**	RAF No. 1212908	RAF	**KL182**		-
10.08.45	W/O Robert **SHANKS**	RAF No. 1319976	RAF	**KJ184**		-
20.09.45	W/O Thomas B. **DRAKE**	RAF No. 943911	RAF	**KJ256**		-

Total: 3

No. 34 Squadron - code EG

No. 34 Squadron was a bomber squadron from 1935 and served in the Far East from the beginning of the war. Since then the only enemy it had faced was the Japanese. In August 1943 the squadron became a fighter-bomber unit, flying Hurricanes, and participated in the heavy fighting of 1944. Even though operational activity decreased, it never stopped and the squadron undertook its conversion on to the Thunderbolt at Wangjing under the authority of 910 Wing. The conversion was done flight by flight so that the squadron could continue to meet its operational requirements. B Flight, along with the CO, S/L J.A. Busbridge, was the first to convert from 9 March 1945 onwards, leaving A Flight to continue its support of ground forces. After having completed its training on Mk.Is, B Flight returned with the first four Thunderbolt Mk.IIs - KJ272, KL178, KL188 and KL252 - on the 19th, allowing A Flight to undertake its own conversion from that date. Two days later, B Flight became operational on T-bolts and the first op was carried out - accompanying Thunderbolts of No. 113 Squadron. The four aircraft were led by W/O Reid. B Flight continued with its four T-Bolts until the end of the month, flying 24 operational sorties. In April the squadron continued its support of Nos. 2 and 20

This photo, while poor quality, is a rare image of a Thunderbolt of 34 Sqn. Note the extra large individual letter, compared to the squadron codes, and the serial, KJ201, repeated on the fin. This was a regular practice in Thunderbolt squadrons in 1945. *(A. Thomas)*

Divisions, initially with the four previously mentioned aircraft, reinforced by KL200, KL204, KL213, KL219 and KL244. This situation lasted until the middle of the month when A Flight returned and more aircraft were received. On the 16th, during a strafing mission, the squadron lost its first Thunderbolt on operations when W/O K.F. Medcalf in KL258 encountered engine trouble after pulling out of dive. Losing power, he was obliged to make a forced landing in the British lines. Although safe, he was injured and was evacuated. The previous day, another Thunderbolt had been lost, when Sgt P. Orton, just posted in direct from the Hurricane training flight, was unable to properly control his machine (KL275) and it ran into soft ground causing the main gear to collapse. This accident proved again that converting from the Hurricane to the Thunderbolt was not an easy task. When the squadron moved to Kwetnge, more sorties were planned and carried out (173 for the month) even though serviceability continued to hamper operations. At the end of the month, among the aircraft in service, in addition to those previously mentioned, were KJ274, KJ328, KJ356/E, KL189, KL201/F, KL224, KL262, KL313 and KL315.

In May, S/L Busbridge relinquished command to S/L G.T.A. Douglas on the first of the month, but Douglas did not arrive until the 26th. Operations were almost discontinued during May, with only twelve sorties flown, as the squadron encountered personnel problems. By the end of the month only nine pilots, all operationally proficient, were able to carry out combat sorties as many other pilots were tour expired and leaving the squadron one by one. As in April, there was also a shortage of aircraft. Since there were not enough for the operational pilots to fly ops, it was simply not possible to make aircraft available for training. In May, however, the situation was reversed with two Thunderbolts per pilot! It was all for nothing, however, as, to make the situation worse, some of the few operational pilots had medical problems – mainly bowel disorders – meaning that the squadron was really not operational even though it officially was. It was a situation S/L Douglas had to handle on his own as nobody at HQ had briefed him about what he was going to find when he arrived.

On 1 June, the squadron moved to Kinmagon in Burma, but flew only 36 sorties, mainly due to bad weather and various diseases with many pilots reported as 'sick'. Fortunately, nine new pilots arrived from No. 8 RFU in good health (!) to rebalance the situation a little. The squadron wrecked a T-Bolt (KL204) during a non-operational flight that month when the engine of W/O E.W. Popplewell's aircraft failed in the circuit obliging him to make a forced landing. The Thunderbolt was destroyed, but Popplewell escaped injury.

The squadron returned to action on a regular basis in July, performing over 200 sorties for the month, harassing the enemy and achieving considerable success against Japanese troops. However, it was not without cost. First, F/Sgt R.S. Neate was posted missing in KJ252 on the 9th when returning from a strafing mission north of Mokpalin. The pilot was thought to have lost control while flying on instruments in cloud. Then, on the 21st, F/Sgt K.G. Dawkin in KJ251 crashed when the aircraft swung on landing on return from a bombing and strafing mission. In July, there was also several accidents, one causing the death of F/Sgt D.S. Murray who was lost on a training flight (KL260) when he crashed following an engine failure. With a lack of experience on T-Bolts, Murray was unable to control the beast and a wing struck the ground and caused the aircraft to turn over twice.

Offensive operations continued until 12 August 1945. The squadron then switched to leaflet drops after the 15th, the last such sortie being recorded on the 30th. Sadly, on the last op for the month, the squadron had to report the death of W/O G.E. Chaney who crashed in flames close to the target after reporting engine trouble with KJ356. At the end of August, the following Thunderbolts were on charge: KL201, KJ252, KJ256, KJ272, KJ328, KJ332, KL183, KL189, KL200, KL201, KL219, KL270, KL281, KL283, KL311 and KL840. The squadron continued to drop leaflets and fly recce flights over ex-POW camps in September with 35 sorties flown. It was during a recce flight that KL189 and its pilot, F/Sgt D.E. Butler, were lost close to the target for unknown reasons. It was the very last operation for the squadron (The CWGC gives the official date of death as 10.09.45, but the ORB reports it occurred on the 11ᵗʰ). No further operational flights were carried out in October and only practice flights were performed. On one of these, the last Thunderbolt was lost when KL841 crashed on take-off on the 9ᵗʰ. The pilot, F/O G.V. Sorrell, escaped injury. The squadron was disbanded six days later after having completed close to 600 sorties with Thunderbolts, all but twelve attributable to the Mk.II.

Summary of the aircraft lost on Operations - 34 Squadron

Date	Pilot	S/N	Origin	Serial	Code	Fate
16.04.45	W/O Kenneth F. **MEDCALF**	RAF No. 1320945	RAF	**KL258**		-
09.07.45	F/Sgt Robert S. **NEATE**	RAF No. 1801115	RAF	**KJ252**		†
21.07.45	F/Sgt Kenneth G. **DAWKIN**	RAF No. 1652496	RAF	**KJ251**		-
30.08.45	W/O George E. **CHANEY**	RAF No. 1318137	RAF	**KJ356**		†
10.09.45	F/Sgt Douglas E. **BUTLER**	RAF No. 1615752	RAF	**KL189**		†

Total: 5

Summary of the aircraft lost by accident - 34 Squadron

Date	Pilot	S/N	Origin	Serial	Code	Fate
15.04.45	Sgt Peter **ORTON**	RAF No. 1452035	RAF	**KL275**		-
04.06.45	W/O E.dward W. **POPPLEWELL**	RAF No. 1087737	RAF	**KL204**		-
12.07.45	F/Sgt Douglas S. **MURRAY**	RAF No. 1603065	RAF	**KL260**		†
09.10.45	F/O Geoffrey V. **SORRELL**	RAF No. 181254	RAF	**KL841**		-

Total: 4

No. 42 Squadron - code AW

No. 42 Squadron was a Hurricane squadron that began the war as a bomber unit until being converted to Hurricane Mk.IVs and IICs in the autumn of 1943. The unit had been fighting in the Far East since September 1942, but on 24 June 1945 the squadron's personnel received the surprise news that the unit would disband on the 30ᵗʰ. The squadron had not flown since the beginning of the month. The following day, No. 146 Squadron, based at Meiktila in Burma, changed identity and became No. 42 Squadron. For the former pilots of 146, it was business as usual as, on 30 June, six Thunderbolts led by the S/L W.M. Souter, the CO, bombed and strafed a village as 146 Squadron and, on the following day, six aircraft took off at 11.00, led by P/O R. Evans (RAAF), to strafe another village, but as 42 Squadron. As far as the squadron personnel were concerned, it was still 146 Squadron and the only worry was wondering if the mail would reach its destination with this sudden change of identity! Over the following days, ops continued while the ground crew painted the squadron codes 'AW' over the 'NA' of 146 Squadron. This could be done rather discreetly on camouflaged aircraft, but on Natural Metal Finish aircraft a big black square was painted over the old code and 'AW' painted in white on that black square. In July the squadron counted 21 operational days and completed 252 sorties without any loss.
In August air activity continued and, up to VJ-Day, the squadron flew ops seven times with S/L Souter leading all but two of them. After VJ-Day, offensive activities were halted, but some flights were carried out, such as a tactical recce on the 18ᵗʰ. One last offensive operation was flown two days later when troops concentrations were spotted. Squadron Leader Souter led twelve aircraft to the area which was bombed and strafed, the T-bolts dropping their 24 500-lb bombs and firing almost 10,000 rounds of 0.50-in ammunition in two strafing runs. That was the last sortie of the month, as Allied combat operations were put on hold pending the official surrender of the Empire of Japan. Small changes occurred within the squadron in September, a month of little air activity with only

Above, Thunderbolt KL315/AW-F, formerly NA-L of 146 Sqn. It was the mount of S/L Souter, the CO, when he was leading 146 Sqn and also when he became OC of 42 Sqn. A black square was painted over 146 Squadron's codes to allow the ground crew to easily apply 42 Squadron's codes. *(A. Thomas)*
Below, KJ357/AW-L, formerly NA-L of 146 Sqn. It was F/O 'Digger' Fraser's favourite aircraft while he was a member of 146 Sqn and remained so when the unit became 42 Sqn (see the 146 Sqn chapter for more details).

tactical recces flown on the 11th, 13th and 17th. Generally, these were to verify suspicious troop movements or to certify if bridges or other infrastructure was still intact. Otherwise, September was quiet. In all, 42 Squadron completed more than 350 Thunderbolt sorties. The last operational Thunderbolts on hand were KJ146, KJ245, KJ246, KJ302/P, KJ318, KJ337, KJ344, KJ346, KJ357/L, KJ358, KL168, KL177, KL225, KL250 and KL315/F. In October, flights were reduced to a minimum but, on the 11th, Sgt Adkins had a bad experience with KJ245. The port tyre burst on take-off, but the pilot was able to get the aircraft airborne and returned to base to make a safe belly landing. Due to the end of the war, KJ245 was not seriously considered for eventual repair and the aircraft was struck off charge. November was also an uneventful month, other than the official announcement of the award of the DFC to P/O Richard Evans (RAAF) and the DFM to F/Sgt Frank Thomas for their time with 42 Squadron. Both had flown and completed most of their sorties with 146 Squadron, a unit most of the older pilots had a strong emotional link with, so it seemed unfair that 42 Squadron received the recognition. The next month, all activity ceased on the 28th and the squadron was officially disbanded on the last day of December.

Summary of the aircraft lost by accident - 42 Squadron

Date	Pilot	S/N	Origin	Serial	Code	Fate
11.10.45	Sgt Robert M. **Adtkins**	RAF No. 1584352	RAF	**KJ245**		-
		Total: 1				

No. 60 Squadron - code MU

By the summer of 1945, No. 60 Squadron was among the very last operational RAF units to still be flying the Hurricane. With totally obsolete equipment, and in preparation for the liberation of Malaya, the squadron was withdrawn from the frontline to begin a conversion under S/L J.B. Wales, who had been leading the unit since May. A new base was chosen, Tanjore, south of Madras, and the move was completed on 10 July. However, once there, the training program was gravely hampered by a lack of aircraft and maintenance equipment. It was therefore decided to send twenty of the pilots to convert at 8 RFU at Yelahanka. The conversion of all 32

A section of 60 Squadron's Thunderbolts flying over the island of Java. In the foreground is KL266/MU-S. It would be one of the last Thunderbolts in service with the squadron. *(A. Thomas)*

Republic Thunderbolt KL882/MU-H with a dorsal fin in natural metal finish in 1946. Note the serial repeated at the bottom of the fin.

pilots ended early in August, the training program possibly being accelerated due to the pilots' high level of experience. No major incidents were reported, but the lack of ground equipment remained an issue in August even with the end of the war. From that point, everything was, more or less, frozen in place waiting for news about the future of the squadron. In early September, the squadron heard that it would be part of the Occupation Force. A first move eastwards took place at the end of September, the unit joining the station at Baigachi, near Calcutta. It then moved to Zayatkwin, in Burma, the following month, with the final destination being Kermajoran, near Batavia, in the NEI, which was reached on the 21st and where 60 Squadron was to share the facilities with 81 Squadron. In the meantime, the squadron was reduced in size, losing many pilots posted away for repatriation and demobilisation. The squadron arrived in Indonesia with the following Thunderbolts: HD243, KJ176, KL187/M, KJ238, KJ260, KJ310, KL211, KL303, KL305, KL317, KL331, KL332, KL336, KL341, KL344 and KL859/T. The first operation in Java took place on the 25th and was to operate over Sourabaya as troops of the 49th Indian Infantry Brigade made a landing there. This operation was flown in conjunction with 81 Squadron. The unit provided six aircraft led by the CO and the operation lasted four and a half hours without incident. Training resumed over the next few days and, during a low-level calibration flight on the 26th, the engine of KL884 developed issues and the pilot, F/Sgt R.L. Beck, was obliged to make a belly landing. The aircraft was a total write-off. Two days later, the squadron was called upon to perform an exhibition flight over Buitenzorg and Banteng where Indonesian extremists were causing trouble. Five runs in varying formations were made over each town as well as dummy dive-bombing attacks from 11,000 to 2,000 feet. A similar operation was flown the next day. However, that was far from enough and the political situation continued to deteriorate with the assassination on the 30th of Brigadier Aubertin W.S. Mallaby of the 2nd Punjab Regiment not a good sign for the future.

Therefore, the number of sorties increased in November and, as was bound to happen, the first shots were fired during an armed reconnaissance when they strafed suspicious vehicles on 1 November. In doing so, the squadron had the dubious honour of being the first to use their guns in Indonesia. From the 9th, the unit also sent some aircraft to Sourabaya, on detachment to support the 5th Indian Division, where major activity was expected after the ultimatum given to the Indonesian extremists expired on the 10th. The squadron flew operations almost every day in November to finish with a total of 114 sorties. During the first days of December, nothing changed, as the detachment of eight Thunderbolts was engaged almost every day in ground support operations while the aircraft left at Batavia carried out more and more routine flights (mainly convoy patrols or covering small scale Army incursions). However on 5 December, Flying Officer E.S Alexander crashed in KL331 after having undeshot the runway, returning from an operation; he escaped injuries. Eventually, the rest of the squadron moved to Sourabaya from the 10th so it could be employed with greater effect. The same day, F/Sgt E.H. Callaghan was taking off in KL303 for a leaflet dropping sortie when the left type burst. The aircraft swung and went into a ditch. The T-bolt was badly damaged and written-off, but the pilot was only slightly injured. However, one week later, the nature of the ground support ops hit home when KJ260 (F/Sgt A.W. Davidson) was shot down by ground fire while acting as No. 2 to F/L J.R. Gibbons during a tactical reconnaissance. He was taken prisoner by the Indonesians and appeared to have been treated well. In January 1946 the squadron was less engaged in operations, so the time was used for training. The two flights alternated each day providing crews and aircraft for readiness. When called for operational duties, the sorties were mostly tactical reconnaissance for the Army even though no specific training in this role had been given to the pilots. Only two offensive ops were flown in January, the first on the 16th with four aircraft led by F/O E.S. Alexander, and the second with four Thunderbolts led by the CO. On the 12th four Thunderbolts led by Pilot Officer H.C. Hume were dispatched for a tactical reconnaissance over Malang, a former Japanese airfield. The Indonesians were known to have taken over the aerodrome and the purpose of the recce was to see what they were doing with the Japanese aircraft. Over the aerodrome it became clear that only elementary trai-

The opposite side of KL882/MU-H.

ning aircraft had been used and the arrival of the Thunderbolts coincided with the turning into wind and taking off of an antique Japanese biplane. The leading T-bolt roared past a few feet overhead and the appearance of the big fighters provoked a great deal of panic in the cockpit of the biplane and it was seen to land abruptly with great force. Sixty-eight sorties were carried out in January.

In February, the squadron began to lose personnel as they were repatriated and, by the end of the month, it was short of manpower. Among the personnel who left was the CO, S/L Wales, who was replaced by S/L D.M. Finn DFC (for service with No. 4 Squadron IAF) from 136 Squadron. The change of command came at the moment when the squadron was a bit more heavily engaged with 104 sorties flown, mainly tactical recces or leaflet drops and a few offensive ops, for the month. On the 13th, returning from a tactical reconnaissance, the engine of KL344 (F/Sgt J. Galloway) lost power causing the aircraft to undershoot the landing. The pilot then decided to retract the undercarriage and make a belly landing short of the runway, sealing the end of the aircraft's flying career with the RAF. March was likewise occupied, but finished with a very efficient offensive operation against a gun position, believed to be 20mm weapons, on the 31st. The op, led by F/O W.D. MacConnachie, was successful as the guns were silenced by strafing and a nearby hut was left in flames. One aircraft was hit by a 20mm shell in the fuselage, something the type could easily sustain, and all four Thunderbolts returned to base. The squadron wrecked a Thunderbolt (KJ265) during an air test on the 27th. The pilot, W/O Albone, thought the engine was not running properly and set up for a hurried landing. In doing so, he misjudged the approach, the aircraft undershot, and touched down heavily short of the runway step, causing serious buckling to the mainplanes. It was never repaired. In April the squadron was grounded between the 16th and 23rd because of recurrent tyre troubles, five having burst on take-off or landing and nine at dispersal. No major damage was caused to the aircraft involved, but a thorough investigation had to be carried out before a major accident occurred. Therefore, the squadron only flew 74 sorties in April (the usual tactical reconnaissance flights or leaflet drops). On the plus side, the release of F/Sgt Davidson, shot down in December and held captive since then, was happily received. During April 1946 the following Thunderbolts were used on operations:

HD243, KJ144, KJ238, KJ292, KJ310, KL187/M, KL209, KL211, KL230, KL266/S, KL273, KL305, KL314, KL317, KL332, KL341, KL859/T and KL882/H.

In May the squadron returned to Kermajoran on the 12th. Before that date the tyre problem had limited air activity. On the operational side, 60 performed convoy coverage on the 15th, 17th, 22nd, 24th, 29th and 31st, alternating with 81 Squadron, the other Thunderbolt unit in the NEI. The shortage of pilots also limited the air activity. The squadron remained in the NEI until December, when they left for Malaya where a new conflict was about to emerge. What happened between June and December 1946 is not known with precision as the pages for this period are missing in the ORB and seem to have been lost some time before 1950. Now the only Thunderbolt squadron in Java since the disbandment of 81 Squadron, it is possible no operations were carried out after July 1946 and the three Thunderbolts lost between July and October 1946 (KL211 on 9 July, causing the death of F/Sgt Ian Macdonald when he stalled on approach, KL314 on 1 October, and KJ363 on 14 October) were lost in accidents during training or test flights. Until the end of April 1946, 60 Squadron flew 673 sorties as per the surviving pages of the ORB. By the end of October 1946, the Thunderbolts believed to be in use were:

HD262, KJ238, KJ292, KJ303, KJ310, KJ329, KL178, KL230, KL266/S, KL273, KL317, KL332, KL859/T, KL876 and KL882/H. Another Thunderbolt, KJ362, was on charge with 904 Wing.

Date	Pilot	S/N	Origin	Serial	Code	Fate
05.12.45	F/O Eric S. **ALEXANDER**	RAF No. 160703	RAF	**KL331**		-
10.12.45	F/Sgt Ernest H. **CALLAGHAN**	RAF No. 1568618	RAF	**KL303**		-
17.12.45	F/Sgt Alexander W. **DAVIDSON**	RAF No. 1683563	RAF	**KJ260**		PoW
13.02.46	F/Sgt John F. **GALLOWAY**	RAF No. 1569488	RAF	**KL344**		-

Total: 4

Summary of the aircraft lost by accident - 60 Squadron

Date	Pilot	S/N	Origin	Serial	Code	Fate
26.10.45	F/Sgt Robert L. **BECK**	RAF No. 1568436	RAF	**KL884**		-
27.03.46	W/O Dennis J.P.F. **ALBONE**	RAF No. 1605053	RAF	**KJ265**		-
09.07.46	F/Sgt Ian **MACDONALD**	RAF No. 1570587	RAF	**KL211**		†
01.10.46	F/O Peter R. **QUILTER**	RAF No. 193000	RAF	**KL314**		-
14.10.46	F/O Roy A. **CAMERON**	RAF No. 181781	RAF	**KJ363**		-

Total: 5

No. 79 Squadron - code NV

Under the leadership of S/L D.O. Cunliffe, No. 79 Squadron arrived at Yelahanka on 26 May 1944 to convert to Thunderbolts. The first aircraft arrived in mid-June, and more by the end of the month, but it was not before mid-July that the first flight could be performed, the time having been spent on lectures and cockpit drill, while flying training continued on the Hurricanes. The last Hurricanes eventually left on the 6th and, one week later, the first Thunderbolt solo was completed. Despite a shortage of spare parts and tools, some flying could still be done. However, because of an accident involving Thunderbolts of another squadron, the aircraft were grounded on the 28th. Training resumed on 14 August. By that time, S/L Cunliffe had been sent to the UK on a Fighter Leader Course, so temporary command had been given to F/L K.G. Hemingway. Cunliffe never returned to the squadron and his position was taken over by an Australian, S/L R.D. May, in December. By mid-September, all of the pilots, besides the new ones, had completed their thirty-hour course and the squadron moved on to Arakkonam with flying commencing again from the 20th. At the end of the month, the squadron had 29 pilots, but only thirteen Thunderbolts on hand. Another move took place on 19 October, this time to Manipur Road.

The unit was ready for operations and, unusually, while 79 was not the only Thunderbolt squadron to fly both marks, it was the only one to have equal numbers of Mk.Is and Mk.IIs (HD187, HD235/S, HD247/K, HD268, HD278, HD291/Z and HD301/R were the Mk.IIs on hand). It was part of 909 Wing, and operations began on the first day of November, and during the month the squadron accomplished 157 ground support sorties (and a few escorts). Logically, half of these were flown by Mk.IIs. Bombs only began to be carried and used at the end of the month, so while 66,000 rounds of 0.50-in was fired, only 42 500-lb bombs were dropped (by both marks). Alongside operations, training continued and, on the 4th, HD187 caught fire just before take-off for a long-range cross-country test. The pilot was able to escape, but the fire crew was unable to save the aircraft. This Mk.II was replaced by another, HD270, a couple of days later.

In December, the Thunderbolt Mk.Is were progressively withdrawn and the squadron was almost fully equipped with Mk.IIs by mid-January. On 8 December there was a change of command with the arrival of S/L May. The nature of ops didn't change and the squadron was fully engaged in fighter-bomber duties with occasional escort duties, mostly for other fighter-bomber units. On the 10th, 79 received orders to strafe Thedaw landing ground. All but one aircraft reached the target area (it had to return early) and, when turning towards Thedaw, near Meiktila, F/O R.A. Grayme (RCAF) in HD278 noticed an 'Oscar' on Meiktila airfield. He orde-

Roy David MAY
Aus. 402204

'Gatty' May, from New South Wales, Australia, joined the RAAF in June 1940. He completed his training in Canada in July 1941 and then sailed to the UK where he attended his final course at No 53 OTU. In October he was posted to No 66 Squadron as a Pilot Officer and then, in December, to No 79 (Madras Presidency) Squadron. Three months later the squadron left for India and sealed May's fate until the end of war. He participated in every action that 79 was involved in during his first tour. He finished his tour in November 1943 as a Flight Lieutenant. Earlier in the year he had the opportunity to make some claims, the first on 25 March, when he damaged a Ki-43, and another probably destroyed on the 30th. These would be his only claims of the war. In the first days of October 1944, he started a second tour with No 258 Squadron as a flight commander but was posted to his former squadron, 79, to take command at the end of November. He would lead the squadron over Burma until August 1945, participating in the liberation of Rangoon, and was then repatriated to Australia. He was awarded a DSO the following month and was discharged in December.

Republic Thunderbolt Mk. II KL231
No. 79 (Madras Presidency) squadron
Meiktila (Burma), summer 1945

Thunderbolt HD247/NV-K was one of the original Thunderbolt Mk.IIs issued to 79 Sqn. It remained in the squadron's inventory until the end of January 1945 and was probably then sent to second-line facilities for a possible overhaul. Its subsequent fate is unknown, but it was somewhat prematurely struck off charge on 31 May 1945. The 79 recorded the greatest RAF number of sorties on Thunderbolts with over 2650, of which close to 2500 were on Mk IIs.

red his section to attack and approached the target at low level. The 'Oscar' was still taxiing. Grayme opened fire at 300 yards and the enemy aircraft blew up and was left burning. Flying Officer E.C. Reed (in Mk.I HD174) fired at another parked 'Oscar' which was claimed as damaged, but was confirmed as destroyed a couple of days later. At Thedaw a 'Dinah' was also fired at on the ground (F/L D.C. Mclean, RCAF, in HD270), but no results were observed due to the gathering dusk. Despite heavy AA, no Thunderbolts were hit. The same places were again strafed the following day, but this time the AA was more accurate and four aircraft were hit, one very badly. All were able to return to base, with the pilot of one of the few remaining Mk.Is, F/O H.M.P. Ives (RCAF), in pain. Squadron Leader May, on his first sortie with the squadron, was hit in the airscrew, engine and hydraulic system and had to make a wheels-up landing back at base. Thunderbolt HD268 was too badly damaged to repair. The tempo of sorties increased from the 23rd with 25 sorties flown that day (all but three on Mk.IIs) and, in all, 272 sorties were flown in December (all but 75 by Mk.IIs). January was very intense and the squadron continued to support the Fourteenth Army in its offensive. Most of the time they were airborne twice a day for bombing and strafing missions against various targets, but it just so happened that 79 also had to carry out standing patrols. That was the case on the 13th with eleven Thunderbolts flying over Meiktila. At the end of their patrol, and after contact was made with the relieving section led by the CO, two 'Oscars' were seen flying low over Onbauk airfield. Calling the sections together, P/O G.H. Hopwood went down to investigate and witnessed one 'Oscar' make a strafing run on a parked Dakota. The two 'Oscars' broke off and headed south before any interception could be made. Hopwood's section could not chase the fleeing Japanese, as the two Thunderbolts were short of fuel, so details of their position were given to S/L May. However, May's section seems to have been too far away to conduct a successful interception and the chase was abandoned. The next day, the squadron was called to provide more patrols and to strafe targets of opportunity. That started with a patrol at 20,000 feet for twenty minutes before they went down to 1000 feet to look at enemy airfields in the area.

KJ233 served with 79 from February 1945 until the end. In the last stages of operations in June, it was usually flown by P/O R.E. Amey (RCAF).

As with HD247, HD235/NV-S was among the first Thunderbolt IIs used by 79 Sqn. It was withdrawn from the squadron's list, in February, just a couple of days after HD247. It was eventually struck off charge on 12 July 1945 for unknown reasons after having been declared beyond economical repair the same day. However, it must be said that having many Thunderbolts in surplus by the summer 1945, many aircraft saw heir overhaul posponed and eventually cancelled and were converted to components as the RAF was being short of spare parts for the type.

They soon sighted four 'Oscars' at Kanguang and these were duly strafed and left burning. Thabukton airfield was also attacked and various derelict aircraft seen. The aircraft returned to base, but on landing HD249 overturned and was badly damaged. The pilot, W/O J.F. Williams, escaped with shock and bruising. Sorties were flown against the Japanese airfields during the following days before the unit resumed ground support for the Army. At the end of the month, the pilots had achieved more than an impressive 400 sorties (representing over 1000 hours on operations and 77 more on training), dropped 175 tons of bombs and fired 169,000 rounds of ammunition.

With over 300 close support sorties flown in February for the Army (and occasional escorts for other fighter-bombers), the month resembled January, but with one sobering difference: the squadron lost its first pilot on operations when, on the 10th, Lt M.G. Hall (SAAF) in HD252 crashed into the target on fire during a strike over Meiktila area support of the 19th Indian Division. More fortunate was W/O R.S. Jack (RAAF) two weeks later when, while attacking a bridge near Mandalay in HD234/X and approaching at low level, the Thunderbolt hit trees causing heavy damage to the mainplane. Jack was able to return to base, but the aircraft was too badly damaged and was written-off the following month. The squadron beat its Thunderbolt record in March with 473 sorties flown, but here too this record came at a cost. On the 22nd, when landing in formation on return from a bombing and strafing sortie over Meiktila, P/O T.R. Lyons (RCAF) in HD301 ran into the tail of HD291 when the latter pulled up short on the runway. While HD291 was able to make a safe landing, KJ301 was unable to do so and eventually crashed. Five days later, 79 lost another pilot, Sgt K. Bullimore in KJ136/B. He was bombing and strafing a village when he was seen to crash into the target in flames. The last two ops of the month were carried out on the 31st and both were led by the CO. The target, Nyaungaye, was attacked with excellent results. After the hard fighting of February and March, combat on the ground became less intense as the Fourteenth Army continued its advance towards Rangoon. The squadron moved to Myingyan North (east of Mandalay) on the 19th where it would mainly be located until the end of the campaign. During April 79 carried out 220 sorties in sixteen days, the targets mainly being Japanese troop or gun positions. On 21 April, while taking part in a second cab-rank sortie of the day, Thunderbolt KL231 (W/O R.S. Jack, RAAF) and KJ267 (W/O J.F. Williams) were caught by surprise by light AA (0-50-in MGs) and Jack was hit. Williams, also hit, could only watch as Jack crashed and was killed as he was hit soon after, but managed to keep the aircraft flying until he did a wheels-up landing back at base. This Thunderbolt was repaired and returned to service. In May the last efforts were made to conquer Rangoon and Operation *Dracula* was launched. The squadron flew fifty sorties in two days and moved forward to Tennant. Over the next six days no operations were undertaken and 79 returned to Myingyan on the 6th. Operations resumed on the 9th, but on a smaller scale and, by the end of the month 110 more sorties were flown, generally to attack isolated Japanese positions as the enemy retreated. The rhythm of operations was rather chaotic and the squadron did not mount fly any between 19 and 29 May. The harassment continued in June. On the 2nd, in the afternoon, five Thunderbolts took off to strafe 200 Japanese at Wami. This operation was marred by an accident when F/O G.A. Stewart (RCAF), while joining up, appeared to misjudge the distance and, to avoid colliding with the rest of the formation, banked steeply and spun in. He was killed instantly. Five days later, with the aim of maintaining support for the Army as it rapidly advanced through Burma, the squadron and 910 Wing relocated to Meiktila.

In July the unit continued to provide support to the Fourteenth Army as the Japanese tried to escape to the east. Close to 250 sorties were flown in July, but rarely involved the squadron at full strength (it only happened on the 17th and 19th). Usually, a flight or a sec-

Date	Pilot	S/N	Origin	Serial	Code	Fate
11.12.44	S/L Roy D. **MAY**	AUS. 402204	RAAF	**HD268**		-
13.01.45	W/O John F. **WILLIAMS**	RAF No. 1264495	RAF	**HD221**		-
10.02.45	Lt Martyn B. **HALL**	SAAF No. 328370V	SAAF	**HD252**		†
25.02.45	W/O Russell S. **JACK**	AUS. 410340	RAAF	**HD234**	NV-X	-
22.03.45	P/O Thomas R. **LYONS**	CAN./ J.93613	RCAF	**HD301**		-
27.03.45	Sgt Kenneth **BULLIMORE**	RAF No. 1623877	RAF	**KJ136**	NV-B	†
21.04.45	W/O Russell S. **JACK**	AUS. 410340	RAAF	**KL231**	NV-V	†
02.06.45	F/O George A. **STEWART**	CAN./ C.90340	RCAF	**KL174**	NV-L	†
28.07.45	F/L William **YOUNG**	RAF No. 123224	RAF	**KJ165**		-

Total: 9

Date	Pilot	S/N	Origin	Serial	Code	Fate
04.11.44	W/O John F. **WILLIAMS**	RAF No. 1264495	RAF	**HD187**		-
29.07.45	W/O Arthur **MAJOR**	RAF No. 1386713	RAF	**HD221**		-
02.10.45	Sgt Harold C. **BROWN**	RAF No. 1807508	RAF	**KJ340**		-

Total: 3

tion was requested by the Army. Some days, however, were busy, like the 17th and 28th when 24 or so sorties were flown each time. Incidentally, on the 28th, F/L Young led a section for a successful first op of the day, but while on approach to land in KJ165, the right undercarriage refused to lock down and Young was obliged to make a belly landing. The aircraft was sent for repair, but it was not fixed, due to the approaching end of the war, and it was eventually struck off charge as beyond economical repair on 11 April 1946. The next day the squadron lost another Thunderbolt during a non-operational flight when HD221, which had been collected the same day, ran into a patch of soft ground that had not been flagged and tipped on to its nose. Here, too, the aircraft was not repaired and was struck off charge on 23 August. While British forces were preparing for Operation *Zipper*, and with most of the squadron stood down, 79 continued to provide support to the Army. A change of command took place in August when S/L May handed his position to S/L R.E. Stout (RNZAF), the official change over being on the 9th. The last offensive operation was carried out on the 20th, when F/L Young led the squadron against a troop concentration spread over three target areas. The squadron fired 17,150 rounds of ammunition and dropped their last 24 500-lbs bombs of the war. Some tactical reconnaissance flights were flown later over suspicious areas, the last two being recorded on 14 September (S/L Stout in KL338/Z and Sgt G.D. Peel in KJ315/K) to give a total close to 2500 sorties flown on Thunderbolt II (and 176 more of Mk I), the highest record for a RAF Thunderbolt squadron. At that time, along with KJ315 and KL338, Thunderbolts KJ233, KJ253, KJ257, KJ291, KJ295, KJ307, KJ340, KJ355/X, KL231/L, KL237, KL263, KL267 and KL280 were on strength. The squadron had been notified that it would be disbanded and many pilots were posted out in the following weeks. Flights were reduced to training. On 2 October Sgt H.C. Brown's aircraft suffered an engine failure and ditched in the river. Brown escaped before it sank and was recused by the occupants of a native boat. Full disbandment was actually postponed until the RIAF was ready to take over. At the end of the month F/L H.A. Rogers took command of the squadron as Stout was repatriated to New Zealand. Training flights continued and in November the squadron was able to log 210.35 hours followed by 111.15 in December. From the 15th, the aircraft began to be flown to 1 CMU and the last two weeks were occupied with preparing for the disbandment that ultimately took place on the 30th.

No. 81 Squadron - code FL

No. 81 Squadron became a Thunderbolt unit when its number plate was transferred to No. 123 Squadron on 20 June 1945. The squadron was led by S/L A.J. McGregor and was working up for the invasion of Malaya. July remained a very quiet month with little flying done, mainly due to logistical issues, so the only event of note was the arrival of the new CO, S/L P.A. Kennedy, who took over on the 16th. Patrick Kennedy had served for a long time in the Far East, particularly with No. 4 Squadron, IAF where he was awarded the DFC. Training resumed with added intensity in August, but soon several accidents occurred. August 3 was a black day. Two Thunderbolts were lost. First, KJ306 was struck from behind by KL195 as it was taxiing clear of the runway and, second, KJ334 flown by the CO, overshot the runway and overturned after an engine failure. Fortunately no personnel losses were reported. Nothing changed until the beginning of October when the squadron was sent to Batavia to help the Dutch restore their sovereignty over the NEI. The squadron was one of two Thunderbolt units there (the other being 60 Squadron). The ferry flight cost one Thunderbolt, KJ255, that belly-landed in an open area near Trengganu, central Malaya, after the propeller's constant speed unit failed. The pilot was uninjured.

The squadron arrived on 21 October 1945 while still under 904 Wing authority (G/C David J.P. Lee). The Thunderbolts on hand at the time were KJ141, KJ148/C, KJ212, KJ226/S, KJ242, KJ288, KJ320, KJ329, KJ363, KL234, KL259/D, KL274, KL295, KL300 and KL875. Four days later, 81 Squadron was sent with 60 Squadron to Sourabaya for a demonstration flight led by the CO. While seven aircraft took off, three had to return early due to technical problems. Nevertheless, this task was useful in preventing any hostile reaction from the Indonesians while Commonwealth troops (elements from the 49th Indian Brigade) landed from the sea. In November things became more serious with various fighting reported across the country. The squadron was called upon to provide support either by demonstration flights or to carry out reconnaissance sorties. On the 8th it was reported that about 500 Indonesians were attacking Rapwi camp (Batavia) and two Thunderbolts were detailed to have a look. Warrant Officer P.R. Watts and F/Sgt W.D. Souter took off at 09.35 and were soon over the camp. Various orbits were made, but nothing was seen around the camp so the section returned to base. However, the landing for W/O Watts (KL259/D) was dramatic as he overshot the runway and overturned in a ditch 100 yards off the end of the strip. Watts was killed in the crash. Batavia was a dangerous place, as besides the ops, all squadron personnel were possible targets (as were other Commonwealth military) and despite orders not to go in to town alone, two crewmen (LAC Geoffrey C. Wilfred and LAC John L. Dawes) were posted missing, believed kidnapped (later found dead), during the month, while another, Sgt Learmoth , was severely wounded and hospitalised with a bullet in his neck. Other incidents like that occurred during the month, such as when, on the way back from Corporal Holland's (who had died from an Typhoid fever) funeral on the 18th, a hand grenade was thrown at the convoy. One person was slightly injured. On the 20th, the squadron was sent to do its real job when it flew a strike to attack buildings at Samerang. Six aircraft, three with bombs led by the CO, S/L Kennedy, and three with guns only, led by B Flight CO, F/L A.V. Naylor, achieved some good results and helped to clean up the resistance in the area. Three days later eight sorties were carried out and one convoy was strafed. Flight Sergeant D.J. Barnston and Sgt Duffy

A line-up of Thunderbolts from 81 Sqn at Kemajoran in the NEI. In the foreground is HD185/FL-O. This aircraft was a real veteran, having previously served with Nos. 258 and 261 Squadrons and was among the first Thunderbolt Mk.IIs sent to the Far East. It was issued to 81 Sqn in November 1945 to use its last remaining hours before its next major overhaul. When it reached the limit, the overhaul was never undertaken and the aircraft was struck off charge at the end of March 1946.

Armed with bombs under the wings, these 81 Sqn T-Bolts are taxiing out, in front of KL187/MU-M of 60 Sqn, the other Thunderbolt squadron of the Wing, for another sortie. The use of bombs was not that common as the eight 0.50-in guns were judged sufficient to deal with most targets encountered at the time.

claimed the destruction of two staff cars, one lorry and a coach. In the early afternoon the CO, who was leading four aircraft, was called to intercept some boats landing large numbers of Indonesians in the NE and NW corners of Lake Ambarawa. Even though the four T-bolts arrived a bit too late, the boats and the last Indonesians still in the area were duly strafed. However, Number 4 in the formation, F/O P.W. Crawshay-Fry in KJ226/S, was too slow in pulling out, struck the sea, overturned and broke up. There was no chance of survival for the pilot. A few more air strikes were successfully carried out by the end of the month, without any loss, but it had become clear by the end of November that the assignment was not a peaceful walk in the park!

In December the number of sorties increased steadily, going from 70 in November to 165, most involving the use of guns and bombs. Some raids were rather deadly for the Indos. For example, no less than 200 casualties were reported after a combined strike force of three 81 Squadron Thunderbolts and three Mosquitos from 47 Squadron attacked enemy positions. No losses were reported even though some light flak (usually 0.50-in MG) was sometimes encountered. In January and February 1946 ops continued, but with less intensity (about 125 sorties carried out each month). On 2 January, twelve sorties were flown to cover a convoy, sections taking turns to ensure continuous support. During one of these, the aircraft flown by F/Sgt C.F. Lambourne had to make an emergency and safe landing at Andir airfield due to engine trouble. Fortunately, there were no serious consequences for the pilot or the

Summary of the aircraft lost on Operations - 81 Squadron

Date	Pilot	S/N	Origin	Serial	Code	Fate
08.11.45	W/O Peter R. **Watts**	RAF No. 1324711	RAF	**KL259**	FL-D	†
23.11.45	F/O Peter W. **Crawshay-Fry**	RAF No. 181944	RAF	**KJ226**	FL-S	†
06.06.46	P/O Gerald F. **Walden**	RAF No. 202862	RAF	**KL249**		-

Total: 3

A Thunderbolt of 81 Sqn taking off with extra fuel tanks under the wings. It carries the ace of spades squadron emblem.

Summary of the aircraft lost by accident - 81 Squadron

Date	Pilot	S/N	Origin	Serial	Code	Fate
03.08.45	W/O Kenneth H.R. **JONES**	RAF No. 1435125	RAF	**KJ306**		-
	S/L Patrick A. **KENNEDY**	RAF No. 122141	RAF	**KJ334**		-
10.10.45	F/Sgt Edwin F. **SMEETH**	RAF No. 1807935	RAF	**KJ255**		-

Total: 3

aircraft. Actually, January was considered the quietest month, from an operational point of view, since the arrival of the squadron in Java. The only complaints were about the weather, January having been particularly rainy, and the lack of variety in the menu! Despite this, morale remained high. Indeed, from a purely operational point of view, the squadron was only tasked with providing cover for convoys or for tactical recces. February was much the same with the squadron entering a sort of routine. That month over 400 hours of all kinds were logged, meaning that the squadron was working at a tempo mid-way between a peacetime unit and a regular unit at war. March was the opposite, as it was the busiest month since the arrival of the squadron in the NEI, with 185 sorties, but there was no change in the assignments – cover for convoys and tactical recces. The only event of note was that the award of DFC to the B Flight commander, F/L Naylor, was gazetted on the 29th. In April the squadron flew close to 450 hours, but with many more hours dedicated to training, as the squadron was often stood down, something that had not happened for many months. This continued in May, helped by the fact that the 23rd Division reduced the number of convoys per week, and also because the task was shared with 60 Squadron. In June 81 flew 433 hours and 134 sorties. On the 6th, while returning from a cover patrol for a convoy, the aircraft flown by P/O G.F. Walden encountered engine trouble and made a perilous landing on the very short airstrip at Tjililitan. To prevent overshooting, the pilot ground looped the Thunderbolt, but the left tyre burst followed by the collapse of the left undercarriage. Fortunately, Walden escaped injury. This was the last major event before the squadron was disbanded on the 30th. The last flights were completed the day before by F/O F.D. Reacroft and F/Sgt Kelly when they landed at 17.45 after two and a half hours covering a convoy. In all, the squadron completed more than 1000 sorties and over 3316 hours in Java. The last known Thunderbolts on strength in June 1946 were: KJ141, KJ148, KJ212, KJ288, KJ320, KJ358, KL178, KL234, KL274, KL290, KL295, KL300 and KL875.

No. 113 Squadron - code AD

This squadron began the war as a bomber unit and fought in the Western Desert, Greece and Burma until 1943 when it was withdrawn to India to be converted to a fighter-bomber unit flying Hurricanes. It became operational on that type in October 1943 and was regularly used against the Japanese until April 1945 when it converted to Thunderbolts. Indeed, after having performed its last Hurricane sorties on the 5th, the unit left Ondaw (Burma) two days later for Wangjing (India) under the command of S/L J. Rose. There they took charge of ageing Thunderbolt Mk.Is. As a turnover of pilots commenced, half of the squadron's pilot roster changed that month, training commenced rather badly as, on the first day, one Thunderbolt crashed. The bad run continued for the squadron when it lost another Thunderbolt on the 15th. It must be said that serviceability of the aircraft remained poor during the month because of a lack of spares and tools to carry out maintenance. The conversion was completed within two weeks, rather faster than the other former Hurricane units, and by the 20th the squadron had moved back to Burma, to Kwetnge , from where it carried out its first operational sorties on Thunderbolts four days later. Until the end of the month the squadron was airborne twice a day, more or less, to participate in the liberation of Rangoon and, in all, 62 Thunderbolt sorties were recorded for April. A last offensive op was flown by six aircraft on the first day of May. A couple of days later two aircraft took off to deliver medical supplies putting an end to the first Thunderbolt deployment for the squadron. A new CO, S/L M. Paddle, also arrived. With the new CO, the squadron was able to replace its ageing Mk.Is with new Mk.IIs (all D-28 or D-30 models). Training continued almost every day weather permitting. The squadron moved to Kinmagan, Burma, in early June where it went into action again, under 908 Wing authority this time (and alongside No. 34 Squadron). Fifty-two sorties had been flown by the 27th. During this period, the squadron lost its first Thunderbolt

Summary of the aircraft lost on Operations - 113 Squadron

Date	Pilot	S/N	Origin	Serial	Code	Fate
23.06.45	W/O John W. **BUTLER**	RAF No. 1550620	RAF	**KL235**	AD-N	-
24.07.45	F/O Alan F. **PROUD**	RAF No. 162392	RAF	**KJ343**		-

Total: 2

Summary of the aircraft lost by accident - 113 Squadron

Date	Pilot	S/N	Origin	Serial	Code	Fate
18.08.45	F/O Colin J. **ELLIS**	RAF No. 163019	RAF	**KL268**		-
07.10.45	Sgt Lawrence L. **SMART**	RAF No. 1809667	RAF	**KJ248**		-

Total: 2

Thunderbolt KL300 was among the aircraft on strength with 113 Sqn during the summer of 1945. After the unit was disbanded, KL300 was later part of 81 Squadron's inventory and among the last Thunderbolts still operational in the middle of 1946. It was struck off charge on 17 October 1946. (Andrew Thomas)

on operations when W/O J. Butler had to land at Taungoo due to a shortage of fuel as he returned from an offensive strike on the 23rd. The aircraft (KL235/AD-N) swung on landing and was too badly damaged to be repairable. Butler escaped injury. The squadron then moved to Meiktila (Burma) on the last day of the month to become part of 910 Wing with Nos. 34, 42, 79 and 261 Squadrons. Operations with the Wing started immediately and by the end of the month 187 sorties had been flown. Only one incident had to be reported when, on the 24th, F/O A.F. Proud (KJ343) had a tire burst on take-off. He was able to successfully complete the op and, on return, he made a belly landing on a disused airstrip near Taungoo where the Thunderbolt was eventually abandoned despite being repairable.

Limited operations continued in August until VJ-Day and, on the 18th, the squadron came under control of 909 Wing at Zayakwin, 25 miles northeast of Rangoon. On the ferry flight a Thunderbolt (KL268) was lost when it crashed on landing (the pilot was not injured). From this point until October, the squadron attacked some isolated Japanese pockets and flew several reconnaissance patrols over POW camps. The last two operational sorties were recorded on 11 September by F/Sgt A.J. Hopkins and Sgt F.A Boyton-Salts. The Thunderbolts known to be part of the squadron's inventory at the time were: KJ245, KJ248, KJ277, KJ326, KJ339, KJ341, KJ343, KL169, KL189, KL223, KL227, KL238, KL294, KL300/R, KL839 and KL877. Until disbandment, which took place on 15 October 1945, the activity of the squadron diminished rapidly, but this did not prevent the loss of one last Thunderbolt (KJ248) on 7 October. The pilot escaped injury following a belly landing after an oleo leg broke and the undercarriage proved impossible to lock down.

No. 123 Squadron - code XE

Reformed in May 1941 as a Spitfire squadron in the UK, 123 Squadron served almost a year as a post-OTU unit until it was sent to the Middle East in April 1942. There, it served once more as a shadow unit for No. 80 Squadron and in October was sent to Iraq to protect the oilfields. Moving to Western Egypt, it began offensive missions in May 1943, but saw little action. It received new orders to move again to the Far East in November 1943 under the command of S/L A.J. McGregor (a Battle of Britain veteran). Regular operations began in 1944 on Hurricanes, mainly in the ground attack role, until May when the squadron was stood down. That is why it was logically selected to convert to the Thunderbolt. Conversion training began in mid-September with the squadron establishment being completed at the end of the month and the unit equipped with Thunderbolt Mk.Is. The working-up was lengthy, however, and the squadron only became operational in December 1944. By that time it was flying the more capable Mk.II, but kept at least one Mk.I (HD106) as a hack and reserve. Even though some incidents were recorded, no aircraft were lost in training during that period. On 18 December the squadron moved to Nazir, India, to begin operations. On the 27th, after midday, many small-scale sorties were flown - defensive patrols, escort to Dakotas, and strafing attacks. The next day, 123 Squadron conducted a major *Rhubarb* on Kudaung Islands where a few targets, including two sampans, were found and strafed. No major incidents were reported in December 1944 or January 1945 except on 27 January when an explosion occurred in the cockpit of KJ239 while it was being serviced by ground crew. One man, LAC T.G. Wilson, was badly burnt and was admitted to hospital for recovery. KJ239 had recently been taken on charge by the squadron and was being inspected before entering squadron service. The month ended with a strike on a bunker position and the village of Salinbaw where a couple of targets were found and destroyed. By that time the squadron

Joining the RAFVR in November 1938 as an Airman Pilot, McGregor was called up on 1 September 1939. Having completed his training in June 1940, he was commissioned and posted to No 504 (County of Nottingham) Squadron and served with the unit in the Battle of Britain.

In late July 1941, A Flight of 504, McGregor's, was renumbered No 81 Squadron and posted to Leconfield where the personnel were kitted out for an unknown overseas destination. They flew to Abbotsinch in Harrows and embarked for Russia on the carrier HMS Argus, which was carrying crated Hurricanes. On 1 September, the squadron flew off in sixes for Vaenga airfield, near Murmansk, McGregor becoming flight commander. Operations continued until mid-November, when 81's pilots began converting Russian pilots on to the Hurricanes. They left Russia at the end of November, leaving the aircraft and equipment behind. McGregor left 81 in April 1942, tour expired. At the end of the year, he was sent to the Middle East and, in January 1943, was posted to No 94 Squadron in Libya as a flight commander. In August, he was promoted to command No 123 Squadron, moving to the Far East later in the year and operating Spitfires and then Thunderbolts until disbandment in June 1945. He then returned to command 81 Squadron briefly in July. He was made a Companion of the DSO in October 1945. Released from the RAF in 1946, McGregor rejoined and eventually retired in November 1976.

Republic Thunderbolt Mk. II HD242
No. 123 (East India) Squadron
Squadron Leader A.J. McGregor
Nazir (India), winter 1944-1945

had already completed more than 400 sorties on Thunderbolts. In January the following Thunderbolts were flying with the unit: HD213, HD215, HD218, HD224/E, HD226, HD242/A, HD250, HD251/P, HD253, HD254, HD255/U, HD256, HD260/S, HD284, HD293, KJ206, KJ239 and KJ241.

If December and January were free of any drama, things changed in February. On the 12th, twelve aircraft, all carrying two 500-lb bombs on the wing pylons and a 110 US Gal tank under the belly, took off at 09.35 to bomb and strafe Lewe II airfield. Shortly after take-off, F/L Roland Bellisle (RCAF) probably reduced his speed in cloud causing the aircraft (KJ263/XE-K) to stall and spin in to the ground, killing its pilot. The eleven aircraft continued the op and returned to base by 13.00. Six days later, the squadron lost another T-bolt when HD251/XE-P burned out at Radnap after having caught fire during run-up. During this phase, fuel from the belly tank ignited and the fire spread quickly before the ground crew could save the aircraft. The run of bad luck continued and on the 21st it was the turn of W/O P.R. Watts to wreck his aircraft (HD224/XE-E). While taking off for a strafing mission, the Thunderbolt hit trees forcing Watts to return to base where he made a crash-landing. March was an intense month with over 300 sorties and more than 1000 operational hours recorded, mainly cab-rank sorties, but this was not achieved without mishap. On the 8th the B flight CO, F/L A.T. Grubb, was part of a formation of four Thunderbolts detailed to carry out a patrol over Pagan and Meiktila when a tyre burst on take-off. The aircraft ground-looped and the pilot escaped injury, but the patrol continued with the other pair. On 1 April, another patrol over Meiktila area was flown and ground targets found between two villages. Small arms fire was encountered during the attack and Sgt M. Chilman had his Thunderbolt KJ260/XE-S when at 100 feet during the strafing run a delayed drop bomb came off and exploded beneath him. He made an emergency landing at Meiktila and after an hasty repair by RAF Commando's, he managed to fly back to base later that day...the aircraft would remain unrepaired until 6 September when a first decison was made and it was stuck off charge, decision immediately cancelled and the airframe was held in reserve until being stuck off charge for good in March 1946. In April the squadron was transferred from 905 Wing to 904 Wing which meant the end of operational activities from the 8th. That day, two cab-rank ops were carried out, one led by F/L A.T. Grubb and the other by F/O J.E. Cliff (RAAF), to mark the end of operational flying on the Thunderbolt by 123 Squadron after close to 1000 sorties. Indeed, after a rest, the squadron was re-named No. 81 Squadron on 20 June 1945 before any new assignments could be formalised.

Summary of the aircraft lost on Operations - 123 Squadron

Date	Pilot	S/N	Origin	Serial	Code	Fate
12.02.45	F/L Joseph L.A.R. **BELLISLE**	CAN./ J.20225	RCAF	**KJ263**	XE-K	†
21.02.45	W/O Peter R. **WATTS**	RAF No. 1324711	RAF	**HD224**	XE-E	-
08.03.45	F/L Arthur T. **GRUBB**	RAF No. 119737	RAF	**HD215**		-
01.04.45	Sgt Maurice **CHILMAN**	RAF No. 1805321	RAF	**KJ260**	XE-S	-

Total: 4

Summary of the aircraft lost by accident - 123 Squadron

Date	Pilot	S/N	Origin	Serial	Code	Fate
18.02.45	*Ground accident*	-	-	**HD251**	XE-P	-

Total: 1

No. 131 Squadron - code NX

This long-term Spitfire unit became a Thunderbolt unit when No. 134 Squadron was disbanded and all of its aircraft and personnel were officially posted to 131 Squadron on 10 June 1945 (itself just reformed after being disbanded). Number 134 Squadron had been stood down for about a month so things went smoothly. While S/L C.G. Ford logically became the CO, the former aircraft of 134 were flown on the 12th to their new base, Ulundurpet, in India, where another Thunderbolt unit, No. 258 Squadron, was stationed. There they became part of 904 Wing. All traces of 134 would soon disappear as the majority of the pilots were posted away and repatriated in June and July 1945. That month, fourteen new Thunderbolt graduates arrived with four experienced pilots to supervise the 'rookies' even though those four pilots didn't have any experience on Thunderbolts. All but one, a South African, Lt G.K. Soderlung, were British.

The squadron struggled with low morale and problems of all kinds in this theatre that had affected the Spitfire training syllabus. Even with new pilots and aircraft, the training program was curtailed by a lack of ground crew and equipment in the third week of July and, when the equipment eventually arrived, much of it had been lost or stolen in transit. By the end of the month things had returned to normal. The training programme for Operation *Zipper* continued with increasing intensity in August. VJ-Day took the squadron by surprise, but, even so, and with the cancellation of Operation *Zipper*, the unit was selected to go to Malaya as part of the re-occupation forces in the British colony. The move took place on 20 September and fourteen Thunderbolts made the trip to Kuala Lumpur led by a Beaufighter. Nothing of note was reported except that the squadron had been temporarily placed under the command of F/L G.M. Smith as S/L Ford had been posted away. The rest of the squadron, including a couple of aircraft and pilots, remained at Zayatkwin, a station the unit had been based at since 11 September. In October, problems continued in Malaya, where the lack of tools and servicing handicapped the normal life of the squadron, while in India W/O J.H.F. James was killed in KL286 on the 2nd. It seems that he had lost control of his aircraft while practicing flying on instruments and crashed near the airfield. He hadn't been able to fly to Kuala Lumpur because his aircraft had been unserviceable. The bad luck was not over for the squadron, however, as it lost another pilot on the last day of the month when F/O J.G. Hanson was killed while conducting an air test in KL179. He suffered a technical problem with the propeller's constant speed unit and attempted to make a forced landing on the airfield. He overshot and decided to go round again. The throttle was open, but a small fire was seen in the area of the exhaust and the aircraft lost height and crashed into a stream leaving no chance for its pilot to survive. On the 8th a new CO, S/L J.R. Graham, arrived. In November things began to improve and almost 200 hours were recorded, but servicing was still shared with 258 Squadron. That month, on the 17th, the squadron was called to show the flag and make some dummy attacks on Northern Malayan villages - the first six aircraft led by the CO and the last six by F/L G.M. Smith. The next day, the operation was repeated, three sections of four aircraft participating in another 'raid'.

On 1 December eight aircraft again flew dummy attacks and demonstration flights. Over the next few days the squadron was tasked to carry out some recces or leaflet drops, but the activity petered out pending disbandment that occurred on the 31st. During the previous days most of the squadron's aircraft were passed on to 81 Squadron which inherited ten former 131 Squadron that month, while 60 Squadron also received some aircraft from the unit. Regarding personnel, all were posted away, many joining 81 Squadron, one of the last RAF Thunderbolt units at the time.

Summary of the aircraft lost by accident - 131 Squadron

Date	Pilot	S/N	Origin	Serial	Code	Fate
02.10.45	W/O John H.F. **JAMES**	RAF No. 1339604	RAF	**KL286**		†
31.10.45	F/O Jeffrey G. **HANSON**	RAF No. 55136	RAF	**KL179**		†
				Total: 2		

No. 134 Squadron - code GQ

Formed in July 1941, 134 Squadron lived the life of the wanderer having served in Russia, the UK again, then Egypt before it was eventually sent to India in November 1943 as part of the reinforcement of the RAF in the region that had been initiated by London earlier that year. For the first half of 1944, the squadron was heavily involved in fighter-bomber operations (cab-rank) with its Hurricanes. It became non-operational in June to await its new aircraft, the Thunderbolt, and moved to Yelahanka under the command of S/L D.K. MacDonald (RAAF). The switch over was slow, however, as the squadron found itself without aircraft for most of August as the first Thunderbolts only arrived at the squadron on the 23rd. The CO made the first familiarisation flight the same day and eight more pilots followed suit. Other Thunderbolts were added to the squadron's inventory over the next few days, including a Mk.I that was only on strength for a short time as eleven were handed over to 261 Squadron on the 31st. As the Mk.I had made a forced landing in that time, the squadron had three Thunderbolt Mk.IIs left at the end of the month! Despite that, close to 90 hours were flown on Thunderbolts in August. Replacement aircraft soon arrived in September and training continued. Sadly, the squadron had to mourn its first death on Thunderbolts when, on the 5th, W/O E.I. Jones, returning from a training flight, was killed when his aircraft turned over on its back at 100 feet and crashed. Another crash occurred three weeks later with HD212, but the pilot, F/L I.L. Lowen, escaped injury and the aircraft was later repaired. Conversion of the pilots was not a major issue in September, but the short supply of spare parts took its toll. For example, the tailwheel's outer cover appeared to be impossible to obtain. Thunderbolt HD275 had to wait until the middle of the month to have its engine changed so was, therefore, unserviceable until then, and HD209 was temporarily used as a stock of spare parts during the whole month. Tyres gave trouble by bursting easily on landing. That led to various minor accidents that cut the number of Thunderbolts available for the conversion program drastically. Therefore, 134 could only count on an average of eight aircraft per day for its task in September, but close to 600 hours were eventually flown. Not so bad considering the problems the squadron had to face. The lack of aircraft and support meant the target

of 30 September for the end of the initial phase could not be reached. On 6 October, the squadron moved to Arakkonam where it practiced dive-bombing. Maintenance was still an issue with a shortage of American tools and equipment. The number of hours dropped to 435 and serviceability was maintained at 78%. Early in November the squadron was ready for action and a move took place on the 9th when the advance party left Arakkonam for Ratnap, south of Cox's Bazar, which would become its operational base from 26 November until the end of April 1945 (as part of 905 Wing). The squadron was equipped with a mixed fleet of Thunderbolt Mk.Is and IIs, each mark equipping, more or less, one flight. For the Mk.II, the aircraft on charge as operations got underway were HD184/W, HD196/B, HD201/Z, HD209, HD210/R, HD219/L, HD277/M, HD281/T and HD282/A (CO's aircraft). However, it was far from the best situation regarding maintenance, but the goal remained the same, swapping the I for the II as soon as possible when enough of the latter became available. The squadron was fully operational and ready from 4 December onwards. The first day of operations was the 7th and the CO led twelve aircraft to strafe Magwe airfield. After one hour, the target was reached and while no aircraft were seen, there was evidence of recent use so the Thunderbolts concentrated their attacks on the dispersal and some areas that could hide aircraft or other equipment. Two days later, 134 was airborne again using bombs for the first time while attacking bridges at Awrama. The attack was followed by a strafing run from 3000 to 2000 feet. Over the next few days the squadron provided escorts to other aircraft (mainly Dakotas) and carried out some patrols. Two offensive ops were recorded on the 12th, 14th and 15th without any incidents to report. Aside from its operational duties, the squadron had to carry out some extra flights, usually test flights, and it was during one such flight that Thunderbolt HD239, recently arrived at the squadron, was lost on the 17th. On return from a long-range test flight, the turbocharger of the engine exploded and caught fire just after landing. The pilot, F/Sgt P.A. Murray, was able to jump out of the aircraft, but the damage caused by the fire was so severe that the Thunderbolt would not be repaired. The next day two offensive operations were flown, one in the morning and one in the afternoon, with bombs and strafing runs hitting the targets. Twelve more offensive ops were flown before the end of the month, the last two on the 31st, without any incidents to report. In all, 290 sorties were flown in December, two-thirds or so on the Thunderbolt Mk.II. January was more intense with 380 sorties recorded and 309,000 lbs of bombs dropped. That can be seen as being a good result knowing that, between the 7th and the 10th, rain prevented any flying. It came at a cost, however, as HD184 was lost on the 5th, possibly hit by AA, during a strafing run. The aircraft was seen to explode as it crashed into the target. The pilot, F/Sgt O'Neill, was presumed to have been killed as no parachute was seen. Some good news was that the last Mk.Is had left by mid-January and, from that point, 134 was fully equipped with the Mk.II (HD196/B, HD201/Z, HD209/J, HD210/R, HD219/L, HD223/Y, HD233, HD235, HD237/V, HD277/M, HD281/T, HD282/A, KJ176/D, KJ178/F, KJ184/H, KJ217/W, KJ231/S and KJ270/P). This number would be soon cut by one Thunderbolt, HD281, which was lost on the 25th when it was seen to catch fire in flight and crash with its bombs while attacking a Japanese position. There was no doubt about the fate of the pilot. The cause of this loss was not determined. That was the only major event of the month.

The same intensity was maintained in February and the squadron was airborne on 22 of the 28 days, flying one or two ops per day in support of the Army. Japanese AA was very active too and many Thunderbolts were hit. On 2 February KJ270 (P/O R.C. Garrett) was badly hit in the wing while attacking Japanese positions and while he managed to return to base, a wing change was needed. The next day the same pilot hit trees at the end of a strafing run in HD237. This damaged the tailplane, but once more he managed to return base. On 11 February 1945, the squadron participated in an escort of Liberators with 258 Squadron. While 258 was lucky enough to engage Ki-43s (one being shot down), 134 didn't engage. In mid-February, 905 Wing was given the task of medium bombing support to 4th and 33rd Corps, the first target for the squadron being the road junctions at Myotha which was

Donald Kevin MᶜDonald
Aus. 402748

'Aussie Mac' McDonald, from Queensland, Australia, enlisted in the RAAF in October 1940. Upon completion of training in Canada, he sailed to the UK where he was posted to the Spitfire-equipped No. 130 (Punjab) Squadron in October 1941, but left in December when posted to the Far East. There, he joined No. 30 Squadron in February 1942 and served for one year before being posted to No. 136 Squadron in April 1943. He made his first claim, a 'Lily' damaged, on 22 May. He moved again in June to No. 261 Squadron. On 20 October he claimed a 'Sally' as probably destroyed. This would be his last claim. He was made a flight commander and, in May 1944, he left 261 to command No. 134 Squadron with a DFC ribbon on his chest. So far, since he had been in the Far East, all he had flown operationally were Hurricanes, but this era came to an end when the squadron converted to Thunderbolts. He led the squadron until April 1945 when he was posted to a HQ position in Calcutta. In October he was made a Companion of the DSO. He left the service in December 1945.

Republic Thunderbolt Mk. II HD282
No. 134 squadron
Squadron Leader D.K. McDonald
Arkonam (India), October 1944

a Japanese forward base for the soldiers defending the Myinmu and Ngazun bridgeheads. A large ammunition dump was attacked on the 22nd. This dump had previously been attacked by the Wing with moderate success, so a new op was ordered. The attack, led by the CO, was more accurate this time, causing a big explosion. Several aircraft were severely rocked and debris hit KJ209, flown by the South African Lt R.R. Aylward, badly, but both the aircraft and pilot returned to base. The aircraft was too damaged to be repaired and was struck off charge soon after. The CO decided, in light of this incident, that, from then on, attacks on all suspected explosives dumps would break off at 150-200 yards instead of 50. The last op of the month was carried out on the 28th with an attack on the supply dump south of Mandalay. During the month no less than 202,455 rounds of ammunition were fired and 112 tons of bombs dropped in close to 320 sorties. The pressure continued in March with 340 sorties flown, over 1000 operational hours, during which 93 tons of bombs were dropped and over 152,000 rounds fired. Most of the sorties were achieved without incident, but on 17 March two Thunderbolts, flown by P/O E.G. Matta (HD196) and F/Sgt J.H. James (KJ254), were hit by ground fire during the morning op, but both returned to base where a third aircraft suffered a left gear collapse on landing (Lt R.R. Aylward – KJ311). Here, however, the aircraft was declared beyond economical repair after an investigation. The next day it was the turn of W/O A. Thomas (KJ214) to survive the same experience when returning from a sortie. The aircraft was not repaired and was struck off charge on 31 May. On 28 March, in the morning, another aircraft was damaged when KJ290, flown by P/O E.G. Matta at 50 feet, was hit by shrapnel from the bombs dropped by the Thunderbolt flying ahead of him (KJ312 – F/Sgt D.G. Axford). The right oleo was damaged and the aircraft returned to base with Cat2 damage. In the afternoon W/O F.H. Gould (RAAF) failed to take-off for another operation, after a loss of power in HD210, and ran into a paddy field at the end of the runway. The pilot escaped major injury, but the Thunderbolt was too badly damaged to consider any repairs. The month ended with the completion of three cab-rank ops involving four Thunderbolts each. All aircraft returned to base safely. In April 905 Wing was involved in attacking Japanese forces now retreating from Meiktila. This battle was considered won by the 8th. The squadron continued to deliver its deadly attacks until the 13th when 905 Wing was disbanded. Transferred to 904 Wing's control, 134 conducted its last sorties of the month on the following day. The op on the 14th was the last one led by S/L McDonald as he was due for repatriation to Australia. Two days later, operational activity was halted. A few days after that, on the 19th, the new CO, S/L C.G. Ford, took over. At the end of the month the squadron moved to Kyaukpyu, located on the Bay of Bengal, with the rest of the Wing (5, 123 and 258 Squadrons). The day before, 134 had wrecked KJ218 while at Radnap during an official mail run. The left brake seized, causing the tyre to burst, and the aircraft turned over. The pilot survived. It was actually the first such accident of the month as the squadron lost a new Thunderbolt, KL196, on 12 April. The right tyre burst on return from a test flight and the

Four ground crew of 134 Sqn RAF loading a 500-lb GP bomb - inscribed with a Christmas message for the enemy - beneath the wing of 'Jungle Queen', a Thunderbolt Mk.II, at Ratnap, Burma.

aircraft swung into soft sand and the nose dug in, damaging the propeller, mainplane and fuselage. The aircraft, though repairable, would be never be fixed and was struck off charge on 11 June 1945.

The squadron was part of Operation *Dracula* in early May and, during the first fortnight of the month, about 110 sorties were carried out, the last ones on the 14th. The squadron was tasked to cover two brigades of the 26th Division. Two Thunderbolts were wrecked during this operation. Firstly, KJ364 overturned on landing when returning from an operation on 1 May. Its pilot, W/O Gould, survived, slightly injured. Secondly, on the following day, KJ198 and KJ275 collided on landing. The latter was destroyed while KJ198 was later written-off. As far as the pilots were concerned, only P/O R.C. Garrett was slightly injured. By mid-May, 134 was using the following Thunderbolt IIs: HD223, KJ144, KJ184, KJ194/N, KJ235, KJ217, KJ231, KJ259, KJ292, KJ324/L, KL173/A, KL195, KL213/P, KL218, KL245, KL246/E, KL329/B and KL339. One month later, it was the victim of the re-organisation of the RAF in the Far East leading up to Operation *Zipper*. The squadron was disbanded on 10 June and all personnel and aircraft became 131 Squadron. No. 134 Squadron flew close to 1580 sorties on Thunderbolts, including about 1450 on the Mk.II, following the conversion to type during the previous summer.

Summary of the aircraft lost on Operations - 134 Squadron

Date	Pilot	S/N	Origin	Serial	Code	Fa
17.12.44	F/Sgt Peter A. **Murray**	RAF No. 1434396	RAF	**HD239**		-
05.01.45	F/Sgt John G. **O'Neill**	RAF No. 1439445	RAF	**HD184**	GQ-W	†
25.01.45	W/O Roy **MacKenzie**	RAF No. 1393402	RAF	**HD281**	GQ-T	†
22.02.45	Lt Reginald R. **Aylward**	SAAF No. 329148V	SAAF	**KJ209**	GQ-J	-
17.03.45	Lt Reginald R. **Aylward**	SAAF No. 329148V	SAAF	**KJ311**		-
18.03.45	W/O Alexander **Thomas**	RAF No. 657766	RAF	**KJ214**		-
28.03.45	W/O Francis H. **Gould**	Aus. 414671	RAAF	**HD210**	GQ-R	-
01.05.45	W/O Francis H. **Gould**	Aus. 414671	RAAF	**KJ364**		-
02.05.45	F/Sgt Charles C. **Robertson**	RAF No. 1559283	RAF	**KJ198**		-
	P/O Richard C. **Garrett**	RAF No. 162303	RAF	**KJ275**	GQ-T	-

Total: 10

The wreckage of KJ364 after its accident. No one can understand why it was a write-off. Fortunately, the Australian pilot, W/O Gould, was only slightly injured.

Summary of the aircraft lost by accident - 134 Squadron

Date	Pilot	S/N	Origin	Serial	Code	Fate
05.09.44	W/O Emrys I.H. **Jones**	RAF No. 1379211	RAF	**HD283**		†
10.04.45	W/O Gerald F. **Walden**	RAF No. 1317873	RAF	**KJ218**		-
12.04.45	P/O Robert H. **Cuthbertson**	Aus. 413355	RAAF	**KL196**		-
				Total: 3		

No. 135 Squadron - code WK

Number 135 Squadron operated the Thunderbolt Mk.I until the liberation of Burma (see SQUADRONS! No. 2). The unit was stationed at Akyab before moving its air element to Chakulia on 17 May to start its conversion to Thunderbolts before the end of the month. On 23 May 1945, a terrible gale passed over the airfield and two of the Thunderbolts (KJ228,and KJ229) were destroyed or damaged beyond repair. The squadron was re-numbered No. 615 Squadron two weeks later.

Summary of the aircraft lost by accident - 135 Squadron

Date	Pilot	S/N	Origin	Serial	Code	Fate
23.05.45	*Destroyed in gale*	-	-	**KJ228**		-
	Destroyed in gale	-	-	**KJ229**		-
				Total: 2		

No. 146 Squadron - code NA

Formed in 1941 just before Japan entered in the war, No. 146 Squadron had remained in the Far East and had flown its Hurricanes from India until 15 May 1944 when the last sorties on the type were recorded. The next month, while under the command of S/L L.M. O'Leary, the squadron was selected to become one of the first two units to convert to Thunderbolt Mk.Is. After having carried out the cockpit checks and drills, the first soloes were recorded on 21 June. During the first week, the number of flights remained low, with an average of three or four per day, but, from the 28th onwards, things became more intense and training was carried out with ten to seventeen flights per day, when the weather allowed, and by the end of the month more than fifty hours on Thunderbolts had been completed. Training was completed on the Thunderbolt Mk.Is and the first operations were flown by that mark even though a handful of Mk.IIs were on strength (HD190, HD203, HD273/N and HD295/F). These were mostly reserved for the CO and flight commanders, or the most experienced pilots, but most of the time they were kept in reserve as spare parts were not easy to obtain. It would appear that those four Mk.IIs had left by the end of the year. It was agreed that 146 would relinquish all of its Mk.IIs for Mk.Is so as to simplify maintenance.

In March 1945 the squadron gave up its war-weary Thunderbolt Mk.Is for brand new Mk.IIs, the exchange complete after a couple of days. By 10 March the unit was ready to return to operations. The Thunderbolts on hand were KJ210, KJ237, KJ293, KJ302/P, KJ308, KJ316/A, KJ321, KJ325, KJ330, KJ332, KJ337/X, KJ367, KL184, KL190/D, KL191 and KL194. However, this change of equipment didn't bring luck for F/Sgt E.A. Cattell who was killed on the 17th in KJ210 while taking off to provide close Army support. He stopped on the runway, having experienced engine trouble, and was hit by the following T-Bolt, KJ367, flown by Sgt R. Bourn who was injured in the process. Both aircraft were written off, signalling a bad start for the unit's Mk.II era. The bad luck continued for 146 as, before the end of the month, Australian W/O M.C. Keightley wrecked KJ308 in a flying accident on the 29th. In April changes occurred at the head of the squadron with S/L Weir relinquishing command to S/L M.W. Hubble, for whom it was his first operational posting, on the 10th. His leadership didn't last long as, one week later, he was killed while leading twelve aircraft to bomb and strafe south of Yengan. For an unknown reason, his aircraft (KL194) was seen rolling to starboard, while pulling out of a dive after having released its bombs, and crashing into the ground. Hubble became the only CO of a British Thunderbolt unit to be killed either in action or in an accident. He was replaced by S/L W. Souter ten days later. April was the worst month for the squadron,

No.146 Squadron was allocated a couple of Thunderbolt Mk.IIs when converting to the type. In order to standardise its flying equipment, it reverted to the Mk.I in October/November 1944. HD295 was one of the few Mk.IIs on strength in October that year and it is seen here wearing the recently approved Thunderbolt identification markings. They do not conform to the size requirements so are probably experimental. They were probably painted by ground crew, in the interim period, while awaiting clear instructions. Despite being a late recipient of the Mk.II, 146 lost ten in 896 operational sorties (one per ninety sorties), the highest loss rate for a RAF Thunderbolt squadron.

losing two more pilots within two days later on. First, W/O M. Keightley, after the crash in March, hit a tree in KJ321 while attacking a rice factory on the 24th and was killed instantly in the subsequent crash. The next day, another Australian pilot, W/O D. Westgarth in KJ325, lost his life when he collided with a Harvard (KF109) of No. 261 Squadron while returning from a cab-rank sortie. By that time the squadron was using various bases in Burma to follow the advance of the Commonwealth troops fighting on the ground. Even with the fall of Rangoon on 3 May, operations continued for a while to harass retreating Japanese forces. The pressure was maintained until the 18th as operations were stood down. During this phase the squadron lost one aircraft (KJ237) when Sgt A. Wallis crashed at base (Myingyan North) after being forced to return due to engine trouble. He escaped injury. After a short rest in situ, ops resumed on the 30th. The next day, F/Sgt D. Layland wrecked KL191 when he crashed on take-off for a bombing and strafing sortie. While less intense, June was a busy month with close to 250 sorties carried out for the loss of three Thunderbolts in operations and another in an accident. The first to be lost was KJ296 on the 5th when it suffered an undercarriage collapse after an air

Summary of the aircraft lost on Operations - 146 Squadron

Date	Pilot	S/N	Origin	Serial	Code	Fate
17.03.45	F/Sgt Edwin A. **Cattell**	RAF No. 700912	RAF	**KJ210**		†
	Sgt Robert D. **Bourn**	RAF No. 1431513	RAF	**KJ367**		-
17.04.45	S/L Michael W. **Hubble**	RAF No. 49742	RAF	**KL194**		†
24.04.45	W/O Malcolm C. **Keightley**	Aus. 416968	RAAF	**KJ321**		†
25.04.45	W/O Donald D. **Westgarth**	Aus. 413463	RAAF	**KJ325**		†
12.05.45	Sgt Allan **Wallis**	RAF No. 1622880	RAF	**KJ237**		-
31.05.45	F/Sgt Derrick **Layland**	RAF No. 1442844	RAF	**KL191**		-
18.06.45	Sgt Peter W. **Hidgon**	RAF No. 1606075	RAF	**KJ293**		†
29.06.45	Sgt Kenneth H. **Trevitt**	RAF No. 1607447	RAF	**KJ190**		-
	F/Sgt Derrick **Layland**	RAF No. 1442844	RAF	**KL265**		-

Total: 10

Two Australians photographed during December 1944 upon their return from a sortie. Left, Kevin Lafferty of Queensland and, right, Ernest A. 'Digger' Fraser. Fraser was tin mining in Thailand and Burma before the war, which explains why he was among the first enlistees in the recently formed Burma Volunteer Air Force, and also one of the few BVAF members engaged in operations during the war. Lafferty had previously flown 33 operational sorties with 610 Sqn in Europe between June and October 1943 before volunteering for overseas service. He joined 146 Sqn in November 1943 and left in February 1945 at the end of his tour.

test. This test was conducted by F/O E. Fraser, an Australian serving with the little known BVAF (Burma Volunteer Air Force) raised by the British just before the war. On the 18th Sgt Peter W. Hidgon was killed in action over the target. He was seen spinning out of cloud and his aircraft, KJ293, exploded upon hitting the ground, possibly after being hit by flak. Two other Thunderbolts were destroyed on the 29th when they, as part of a formation of six T-Bolts led by F/O Fraser, collided while landing after successfully completing an op. Sergeant K.H. Trevitt (KJ190) was lucky to escape injury, but F/Sgt D. Layland (KL265) was injured in the collision and had to be taken to hospital. The next day, S/L Souter took off at 07.55 with five other T-bolts to carry out a strafing operation on a village called Shawbon. When the formation landed three hours later, it was the end of the official existence of 146 Squadron as it became No. 42 Squadron the next day. It had completed close to 2600 sorties (including 900 on Mk.IIs), the highest record after No. 79 Squadron, meaning that had the unit identity not changed, the squadron would have recorded the greatest number of sorties on Thunderbolts in the RAF!

Summary of the aircraft lost by accident - 146 Squadron

Date	Pilot	S/N	Origin	Serial	Code	Fate
29.03.45	W/O Malcolm C. **Keightley**	Aus. 416968	RAAF	**KJ308**		-
05.06.45	F/O Ernest A. **Fraser**	BVAF No. 1037	(Aus)/BVAF	**KJ296**		-
			Total: 2			

Thunderbolts of 261 Sqn on a forward airstrip near the Burma front in December 1944. In the foreground, FJ-X is believed to be HD246. The serial was masked with mud or clay (probably for censorship reasons). The aircraft behind was not censored.

No. 261 Squadron - code FJ

No. 261 Squadron was one of first two units to convert to the Thunderbolt. This Hurricane unit had been in the region since January 1943 and, in June 1944, it had been led by S/L R.E.A. Mason since May. The first flights took place on 24 June and the squadron used the very first Thunderbolt Mk.Is with the Curtiss propeller. The training program was intense and by the end of the month 115 flights had been successfully completed. Training continued in July and August and it was during the latter that the pilots commenced the last part of their training (air-to-ground firing). The squadron moved to Arakkonam, India, on the 15th once training was finished. Almost 400 hours were flown that month including some on the first Mk.IIs allocated to the squadron, HD195 and HD240. On 2 September, the squadron flew to Kumbhirgram where it would become operational. However it was still flying on mixed fleet of Mk.Is and Mk.IIs with only half a dozen of the latter on strength (HD188, HD195, HD197, HD199, HD202, HD211 and HD240). Routine flights, particularly sector recces to familiarise the pilots with the local landmarks, were carried out during the first days of the month. On 11 September, returning from one such flight, F/Sgt F.W. Richards landed first in a Mk.I (HD178) and mistook the third taxi track for the fourth one. He turned across the runway to reach it and it was at that moment that his wingman, F/Sgt W.I. Macdonald struck Richards' aircraft with his Mk.II (HD188). Both pilots suffered concussions and abrasions and both aircraft sustained heavy damage. The Mk.I was declared non-repairable at once, but HD188 was considered for repair before eventually following the same path on 28 September.

On 16 September, the first operation on T-bolts was carried out when three aircraft led by the CO strafed and bombed a target. Two of the Thunderbolts were Mk.IIs (HD240 flown by the CO and HD211 flown by F/L R.H. Fletcher, B Flight CO). All aircraft returned to base. On 21 September the CO took HD197 for a test flight with long-range tanks. After he had been airborne for about ten minutes his engine cut at 3000 feet and he was obliged to make a forced landing with the wheels up. At the moment of impact, S/L Mason used his left hand to brace himself and badly injured it. He was admitted to hospital and temporary command was given to F/L R.H. Fletcher. By the end of September, more than 100 sorties had been completed, half by Mk.IIs. More Mk.IIs arrived at the squadron during the month (HD185 and HD186), progressively replacing the Mk.Is, but were soon cut by one when HD240 was lost in an accident on 30 September. It was actually lost outside of the squadron's activity, having been loaned to an American pilot (Lt R. Ekins, 90th FS), with the authorisation of the AOC, for a flight to Tikawk Sakan in Burma. In October the RAF concentrated its attacks around Rangoon and 261 was part of this. The proportion of Mk.IIs increased in October and, from the 22nd onwards, all of the sorties were flown by Mk.IIs. The aircraft on charge at the time were HD183, HD185, HD186, HD190, HD196, HD199, HD202, HD203, HD218, HD231, HD241, HD246, HD258, HD273, HD286 and HD295. Some administrative changes took place during the month with a new establishment of thirty pilots (only on paper for a while) and the formation of No. 7261 Service Echelon that absorbed most of the ground staff. November opened with the squadron continuing its operational efforts with attacks on the Japanese airfields at Meiktila and Heho. Generally, on return from these ops, the pilots would attack targets of opportunity, and considerable success was obtained against railway trucks, derricks, buildings or other motor transport vehicles. For a change, on the 6th, ten Thunderbolts were scrambled against enemy aircraft. After patrolling for a few minutes the disappointed pilots were ordered to return to base. Two days later, on the 8th, the squadron was requested to carry out standing patrols in the Kalaymyo-Mawlaik-Tiddim area. While Japanese aircraft were reported, no contact was made. Some escorts were also provided to Dakotas from the 11th onwards before a halt in operations was made between the 18th and 21st in preparation for the move forward to Wangjing. Operations resumed on the 22nd, initially providing escorts, but returning to ground support from the 24th. On the following day, F/O N.W. Faircloth and W/O R.J. Owen, being part of a formation of eleven aircraft attacking Heho, shared in the destruction of a 'Dinah' hidden under netting. On the 28th W/O D.D. Cowper (RAAF) was taking off on a practice flight with long range tanks when his aircraft, HD261, swung violently to the left, shortly after he had begun his run, and struck another Thunderbolt parked on the edge of the runway. The undercarriage then collapsed and Cowper careered along the ground before the aircraft came to rest in flames. Cowper managed to get out in time, with slight burns to his arms, but nothing could be done to prevent the total destruction of the Thunderbolt. At the end of the month the squadron had recorded over 200 sorties during which 18,000-lb of bombs had been dropped and more than 70,000 rounds of ammunition expended.

In December 261 continued its support of the Fourteenth Army advancing towards the Irrawaddy. Some escorts were also provided for Dakotas supplying the British troops, but no Japanese aircraft were encountered during the entire month. As proof of the intensity of the support provided, the number of sorties reached 245 and 33,500-lb of bombs were dropped along with 108,250 rounds of 0.50-in fired. However, that cost a pilot when Warrant Officer T.H. Cambridge (RAAF) was shot down by ground fire on 21 December immediately after a strike on a Japanese camp near Gangaw. Early in the month, F/L Fletcher officially assumed command of the squadron, and was promoted to squadron leader, once it became clear that S/L Mason, injured in September, would not be returning.

In January, the Allied advance really began to get underway and pressure on the Japanese increased at the same time. The squadron continued to be called in support of the Fourteenth Army and around 380 sorties were carried out. Close to 600 bombs were dropped and 112,200 rounds of ammunition fired. No losses, either operational or accidental, were reported. In February the

Thunderbolt FJ-N under maintenance and being serviced in the open for the next operation that would require the extra fuel tanks being prepared.

Thunderbolt KL849, an aircraft of the final batch, is believed to have been issued to 261 Sqn in June or July 1945 and became the mount of the new CO, S/L J.R. Graham, who chose to use the letter 'G' (for Graham) as the aircraft's individual letter. (*A. Thomas*)

battle for central Burma entered its critical and decisive phase, especially, as far as 261 was concerned, over the bridgeheads over the Irrawaddy River. On 1 February 1945, while attacking Meiktila, the squadron lost its B Flight commander, F/L 'Ron' Rees, when he was shot down in flames over the target. He was a long serving member of the squadron, having joined the unit in September 1942 as a sergeant. Another aircraft was lost on the 18th when Sgt Key's Thunderbolt was hit by shrapnel from ordnance exploding on the ground. He managed to force land in enemy territory, but was taken prisoner. He escaped, but was captured again only to escape a second time and return to 261 four days later! The daily number of sorties was maintained during February, but the pilots had more opportunities to use their guns with close to 180,000 rounds of fired while the number of bombs dropped was the same as in January.

In March the squadron performed around 470 sorties, a record to date. All of the ops were centered in the Mandalay-Meiktila-Myingyan triangle. Practically every task carried out by the squadron was to provide close support to the Fourteenth Army operating in the area. The targets could be enemy (under bunkers or not) machine guns nests, troop concentrations and/or supply dumps. With feedback from the ground, the results obtained were generally excellent, but, from the pilots' point of view, the task was a bit monotonous. On 20 March 261 participated (with 79 Squadron) in the attack on Fort Dufferin that proved to be the culmination of the Allied effort to capture the city of Mandalay. When March ended, the squadron had dropped a record 874 500-lb bombs and fired close to 422,000 rounds of ammunition. More than 1236 hours had been flown, all but 75 on operations, there being little time for any training or test flights and, when the squadron was off ops, rest was the priority as flying fatigue began to appear towards the end of the month. This intensive operational effort was not without its setbacks. On 5 March, F/Sgt D.R. Phillips' aircraft exploded during his bombing dive for unknown reasons. The target was not defended by AA, but he was seen to crash in flames. He was killed instantly. As this incident had occurred in the past with other squadron Mk.IIs, and in other Thunderbolt squadrons, an investigation was launched by headquarters. Limitations on the angle of the dive during attacks until the cause could be determined. The intensity of the operations had a big impact on serviceability which dropped to a daily rate of barely ten aircraft by the end of the month (25% less than the end of February). In April operational effort was limited almost entirely to a series of patrols carried out by A Flight from Sinthe under 907 Wing control, while B Flight remained at the squadron's base of Wangzing. Therefore, the number of sorties was reduced to 220 for the entire squadron. As for A Flight, the primary object of these patrols was to supply dawn and dusk cover for elements of the Fourteenth Army advancing down to the Central Burma Plain east of the Irrawaddy. Little happened, expect on the 20th when Thunderbolts (F/L W.E. Pearce and W/O F.B. Handley) were called from their patrols to intercept ten Japanese 'Oscars' reported in the vicinity. However, Spitfires from 152 Squadron were the first to make contact, claiming one 'Oscar' in the process. The T-bolts missed the chance to increase their tally that day. The monotony of those patrols was sometimes interrupted to conduct some strafing and bombing op, but these were much more dangerous as F/Sgt D.O. Grady was shot down and killed on the 14th. Acting as wingman for F/O H.A. Sorenson (RCAF), Grady attacked various targets while conducting a recce south of Shwemyo. A first attack on an ammunition dump was conducted without incident, but over the next target Grady hit trees on his second run and his aircraft was badly damaged. He managed to gain 100 feet and, under his leader's instructions, headed north. However, after a couple of minutes, he reported that his windscreen was covered with oil and the engine temperature was going off the dial. Therefore he made a crash landing with the Thunderbolt almost totally engulfed in flames. He was seen jumping from the cockpit, possibly injured by burns, and seen to start walking northwards. F/O Sorenson immediately reported the crash and there was a good chance of recovery as friendly ground forces were only twelve miles away. However, nothing was heard from Grady afterwards and he was posted missing. On 22 April 910 Wing (79, 146 and 261 Squadrons) moved forward to Myingyan North where A Flight arrived two days later. However, this move, and the change in climate, from temperate weather to excessive heat, led to enteric illness among many personnel. Furthermore, 261 was involved in dramatic accident on the 25th when a Thunderbolt of 146 Squadron collided with 261's Harvard, KF109 flown by W/O G.L.Scudamore, killing both pilots. In May the expected defence of Rangoon by the Japanese failed to materialise and only 115 sorties were carried out. The arrival of the monsoon soon after the recapture of Rangoon also hampered operational activity. In the first week of May the squadron operated from the advanced field 'Tennant' which proved to be unsuitable. By the end of the month, the squadron had the following Thunderbolts on strength: KJ152, KJ158, KJ170, KJ195, KJ200, KJ225, KJ236/A, KJ244, KJ261, KJ273, KJ282, KJ283/N, KJ297, KJ331, KJ335/W, KJ359 and KL239.

It is not possible to know in detail the air activity for June 1945 as this month is absent from the Operations Record Book. There was a change of command with S/L J.R. Graham taking over on an unspecified date. It is known, however, that the squadron was withdrawn from operations on 18 June, to prepare for Operation *Zipper*, and was placed under 904 Wing authority. At least 2100 sorties had been flown by Thunderbolt IIs (for a total of close to 2200 when including the Mk.I). Based at Tanjore from 1 July, training was scheduled to start with completion set for 25 August. However, training only started on 20 July owing to prolonged delays during the move from Burma. By the end of the month less than 200 hours had been flown. Problems regarding the pilots arose as well with fourteen of them being posted to the squadron in July, seven of whom had no Thunderbolt experience. Three of them were so lacking in experience that they were referred to HQ for disposal. This turnover was needed to replace the pilots who were at the end of their tour and to cover the repatriation of RCAF and RAAF personnel. Early in August, the squadron received notice that the date of completion of preparations for Operation *Zipper* was postponed from 25 August to 12 September, much to the relief of squadron personnel who thought the earlier date was too soon. With the Japanese surrender, things changed again, and all air activity was scaled down so that at the end of the month the squadron had flown 238 hours. One Thunderbolt, KJ261, was wrecked on the 21st when it overshot on landing. The pilot escaped injury. Operation *Zipper* was cancelled and 261's fate became uncertain for a couple of weeks as it was considered for the occupation forces. However, notification of disbandment arrived on 5 September and it came into effect on 26 September.

Summary of the aircraft lost on Operations - 261 Squadron

Date	Pilot	S/N	Origin	Serial	Code	Fate
21.12.44	W/O Thomas H. CAMBRIDGE	AUS. 410213	RAAF	KJ232		†
01.02.45	F/L Ronald L. REES	RAF No. 177417	RAF	KJ179	FJ-T	†
18.02.45	Sgt Bernard R. KEY	RAF No. 1615593	RAF	KJ175		-
05.03.45	F/Sgt Denis R. PHILLIPS	RAF No. 1317412	RAF	KJ227		†
14.04.45	F/Sgt Donald O. GRADY	RAF No. 1607363	RAF	KJ192		†

Total: 5

Summary of the aircraft lost by accident - 261 Squadron

Date	Pilot	S/N	Origin	Serial	Code	Fate
11.09.44	F/Sgt William I. MACDONALD	No. 1552821	RAF	HD188		-
30.09.44	Lt R. EKINS		USAAF	HD240		-
28.11.44	W/O Donald D. COWPER	AUS. 409879	RAAF	HD261		-
21.08.45	W/O Frederick B. HANDLEY	RAF No. 963718	RAF	KJ261		-

Total: 4

No. 615 Squadron - code KW

This unit became a Thunderbolt squadron by renumbering No. 135 Squadron on 10 June 1945, the former 615 being disbanded the same day. The former No. 615 Squadron had been a Spitfire unit and S/L L.C.C. Hawkins, the former 135 Squadron CO, continued his role at the head of the new unit at its new base at Vizagapatam, India. Contrary to the other renumbered units, 615 Squadron was built from new British personnel (except P/O F.R Lydecker, an American, and Lt M. Briscoe, a South African), mostly NCOs, as many Dominion pilots were part of the repatriation process. The aircraft were the Thunderbolt Mk.Is 135 Squadron had used, but these were soon phased out and replaced by late model Thunderbolt Mk.IIs on which the squadron code letters 'KW' were applied. As part of 905 Wing, 615 Squadron had been selected to take part in Operation *Zipper*. For this, an intensive program of training was carried out from the beginning of July 1945 onwards due to the fact that many inexperienced pilots had joined the squadron and further training on type was necessary to bring the squadron up to operational standard. In July more than 200 hours of training flights were carried out, but not without problem. On 10 July, Sgt W.G. Wareham was killed in KL214 while returning from a formation sortie. He was overwhelmed by what was required to set up the aircraft for landing, being too late in doing the right thing each time, and consequently hit a tall palm tree and crashed. This crash highlighted the lack of training of some of the young pilots who were ultimately unable to master the Thunderbolt. On the 25th, Hawkins relinquished command to his A Flight commander, F/L P.J. Anson.

In August training continued, but the squadron lost another aircraft. Early in the morning at 7.30, Sgt D.H. Philpott had taken off for a cross-country and aerobatics practice when, in trying to do a loop, he failed and entered an uncontrollable spin. He abandoned the aircraft at 6000 feet. Once again, the inexperience of the pilot on the type was the main cause of the accident. Despite this, the squadron continued to practice almost every day as weather permitted and an average of twenty sorties per day were recorded up to VJ-Day. Up to that date more than 230 hours were flown and, except for the news of the Japanese surrender, no events of note were reported until the end of the month. However, training, mainly cross-country flights, was maintained and at the end of the month 466 hours had been recorded and 137 100-lb bombs dropped. In September things changed radically when it was announced, on the 6th, that the squadron was to be disbanded and returned to its roots by being reformed as an Auxiliary squadron. Four days later S/L Anson left and the hours flown reduced. During the following days, the pilots began to ferry their aircraft to Maintenance Units for storage. The official disbandment occurred on the 25th. In all the squadron recorded more than 750 hours on Thunderbolts, lost two aircraft and one pilot.

Summary of the aircraft lost by accident - 615 Squadron

Date	Pilot	S/N	Origin	Serial	Code	Fate
10.07.45	Sgt William G. **Wareham**	No. 1605629	RAF	**KL214**		†
03.08.45	Sgt Derreck H.B. **Philpot**	RAF No. 1802990	RAF	**KL299**		-

Total: 2

The new 615 Sqn, being one of the last squadrons to receive the Thunderbolt, was equipped with the latest variant of the Mk.II, such as KL856 seen here. KL848, KL850, KL879 and KL883 are also known to be from this batch.

Training on the Thunderbolt

The first task the RAF had to carry out was to convert Hurricane pilots onto Thunderbolts. A special unit in 225 Group was formed on 20 June 1944, No. 1670 (Thunderbolt) Conversion Unit, based at Yelahanka in India and its command was initially given to Squadron Leader P.J.T. Stephenson, formerly OC No. 607 Squadron. The first Thunderbolts were rapidly re-assembled and the unit was able to begin training of the first two units, Nos. 146 and 261 Squadrons, immediately. The plan was to continue to convert the units two at a time. While the ground crew was trained on an aircraft much more complicated than the Hurricane, the pilots had to follow a flight training regime comprising of the following syllabus:

One sector recce and familiarisation flight
One section formation flight
Four squadron balbo flights
One individual low-level bombing flight
Two section low-level bombing flights
Three 45-degree dive-bombing attacks from 10,000 feet (releasing at 3500 feet)
One air-to-ground firing flight
One air-to-air dogfight flight (with cine cameras)
One cloud flying flight
One low-level cross-country flight (400 miles)
One low-level cross-country flight (1000 miles)

That represented about 21-22 hours of flight with two hours on a Harvard for instrument flying. So a Hurricane pilot should be able to convert to the Thunderbolt in about 25 hours whatever experience he already had! Easy to

Flight Lieutenant Don Aurisch, a New Zealander in the RAF who later transferred to the RNZAF in January 1945, was among his country's most experienced Thunderbolt pilots. For seven months, during 1944 and 1945, he was in command of a Thunderbolt Flight with 1670 CU at Yelahanka and later with 8 RFU. He had previously completed two tours of operations with Nos. 258, 615 and 17 Squadrons in Europe and the Far East. *(D. Aurish via P. Sortehaug)*
Below, a Thunderbolt Mk.II, coded 'X', is believed to belong to either 1670 CU or 8 RFU. Those units used single letters only to identify their aircraft. *(via A. Thomas)*

say, but maybe not so easy to do as the Thunderbolt had a gross weight double that of the Hurricane. Mastering the Thunderbolt, which also had the propensity to spin, was more difficult than expected and many pilots found the Thunderbolt tricky to handle. It was far from easy to tame, especially for just graduated pilots. As the Mk.I was available in greater numbers when 1670 CU was formed, the presence of the Mk.II in these units remained limited. However, the use of at least HD206, HD207, HD220, HD221, HD228, HD275, HD297, KJ286 and KL176 is confirmed. The first Thunderbolt Mk.II seems to have been taken on charge by 1670 CU at the end of August 1944. The unit continued to convert pilots until 24 January 1945 when it was renamed No. 8 Refresher Flying Unit (RFU), continuing in the same role. It logically inherited the aircraft from 1670 CU, including most of its Mk.IIs, and further Mk.IIs were progressively added to the inventory (those known were HD196, HD275, KJ215, KJ286, KL193, KL226, KL233, KL254, KL284, KL298 and KL838). Having no further need to convert or refresh pilots for the decreasing Thunderbolt units, 8 RFU ceased to exist on 24 November 1945 and its personnel were posted to No. 3 RFU where a limited number of Thunderbolts were used (use of KJ174, KJ256, KL287, KL343 and KL842 is confirmed).

Summary of the aircraft lost by accident - 8 RFU

Date	Pilot	S/N	Origin	Serial	Code	Fate
27.03.45	F/O Raymond R. **WILSON**	CAN./ J.85702	RCAF	**KL247**		-
21.04.45	Sgt Norman **MCPHERSON**	RAF No. 2203442	RAF	**HD207**		-
12.05.45	F/O Raymond R. **WILSON**	CAN./ J.85702	RCAF	**KL838**		-
04.06.45	Sgt George **HERITAGE**	RAF No.1583748	RAF	**KL284**		-
21.07.45	W/O William S. **ELLIS**	RAF No. 1498256	RAF	**HD220**		-
11.08.45	P/O Robin R. **MASON**	RAF No. 163315	RAF	**HD196**		-
	P/O John M. **WRIGHT**	RAF No. 163314	RAF	**KL193**		-

Total: 9

The Thunderbolt was also used by No. 73 OTU based at Fayid in Egypt. In 1944 this OTU provided training for Hurricane units in the fighter-bomber role for both the Far East and Mediterranean theatres. As the basic role remained the same, the Thunderbolt was added to the OTU's inventory at the same time as the Thunderbolt entered RAF service. A mixed fleet of Thunderbolts was sent to Egypt once re-assembled in India, keeping the camouflage applied by the factory in the USA. With the absence of any records, it is difficult to know exactly how many Thunderbolts Mk.IIs were actually sent to Fayid. There were around fifty sent from mid-summer 1944, alongside the Mk.Is, once they were delivered to India. A few more were added to the inventory later on to make up for attrition. The Mk.IIs, like the Mk.Is, served until the OTU was disbanded on 25 September 1945, and the surviving aircraft were stored until all were struck off charge on 14 March 1946 and scrapped.

Wing Commander P.J. Stephenson posing in front of his Thunderbolt Mk II, KL330/PJ-S while serving with 73 OTU during the summer of 1945. *(A. Thomas)*

Patrick Joseph Thomas STEPHENSON

RAF No. 81343

'Paddy' Stephenson, from Dublin, joined the RAFVR in September 1938 as an airman pilot and was still under training when war broke out. In June 1940 he was posted to No. 607 (County of Durham) Squadron flying Hurricanes and participated in the Battle of Britain. On 15 September he shot down a Do17 then collided with another and bailed out. The Dornier crashed so he opened his score with two confirmed victories. In December 1940 he was briefly posted to Defiant-equipped No. 96 Squadron on formation, but returned to 607 before the end of the year. In June 1941 he was posted out for a rest, but was back with 607 in September. In December he became a flight commander and made his second claim, a Bf109 destroyed, on the 5th. He accompanied the squadron to India and in April 1943 he assumed command, relinquishing the position in March 1944. In the meantime, a DFC was awarded in September 1943 and on 15 January 1944 he made his final claim, a probable Ki-43, while flying a Spitfire Mk V, a type recently introduced to the Far East. His final score was three confirmed victories and one probable. No further operational positions followed before the end of the war and ended with 73 OTU in Egypt as a wing commander flying to convert pilots for service in the Far East. He stayed with the RAF before resigning in July 1955.

Republic Thunderbolt Mk. II KL330
No. 73 Operational Training Unit (OTU)
Wing Commander Patrick J.P. Stephenson
Fayid (Egypt), spring-summer 1945

Two views of a black painted Thunderbolt KJ348 as used by Group Captain Carey while OC 73 OTU at Fayid, Egypt. *(Andrew Thomas)*

Enlisting in the RAF as an aircraft apprentice in 1927, Carey passed out as a metal rigger three years later. In 1935, he applied, and was accepted, for pilot training, joining No. 43 Squadron as a non-commissioned officer upon completion. He was still with the squadron when war broke out. It didn't take long for him to open his score, sharing in the destruction of an He111 on 30 January 1940. Other claims followed during the next few weeks and, in March, he was awarded the DFM before being commissioned in April and heading to No. 3 Squadron to participate in the Battle of France. In four days, he made 18 claims before being shot down and wounded on 14 May. Early in June, he was evacuated to England where he learned he had been posted missing and awarded the DFC and Bar the same day. At the end of June, he rejoined 43 and participated in the Battle of Britain, adding a further 15 claims to his scoreboard before again being wounded in action on 18 August. He remained out of the fight until the beginning of October. In November, he was rested, but started another tour of operations in February as a flight commander with No. 245 Squadron. In August 1941, he was given command of No. 135 Squadron upon its formation and, in December, sailed with the squadron for the Far East, arriving in Burma in January 1942. In February, he was successful against Japanese aircraft and soon after was promoted to become Wing Leader of No. 267 Wing, adding a second Bar to his DFC the following month. His final victory was on 25 October, when he got a possible 'Oscar' to bring his tally to 28 confirmed victories (three shared), seven unconfirmed or probables, and eight damaged. At the end of the year, he left 267 Wing. No further operational positions followed and, as a group captain in November 1944, he was given command of No. 73 OTU in Egypt. After the war, Carey continued his career with the RAF before retiring in June 1960.

Republic Thunderbolt Mk. II KJ348
No. 73 Operational Training Unit (OTU)
Group Captain F.R. Carey
Fayid (Egypt), spring 1945

Two of 73 OTU's Thunderbolts waiting for their next training flight. In the foreground, Thunderbolt '4' belongs to the 'KJ' serial sequence while, behind, Thunderbolt '3' belongs to the 'KL' sequence. Below, JK159/30 in flight. No. 73 OTU, as with all overseas OTUs, used a number to identify its aircraft. The Thunderbolt was far from an easy bird to master for fresh graduates who had arrived directly from Harvards, as proven by the high number of pilots killed per number of accidents (well above other aircraft types). The opposite was the case regarding the refresher courses where the pilots gained experience on other combat aircraft like the Hurricane or Spitfire. These courses proved a more favourable step to the Thunderbolt.

Date	Pilot	S/N	Origin	Serial	Code	Fate
13.01.45	F/Sgt Arthur A. **White**	Aus. 432912	RAAF	**KJ169**		†
23.01.45	F/Sgt Stanley **Mumford**	RAF No. 1801489	RAF	**KJ162**		-
30.01.45	Sgt John R.C. **Small**	RAF No. 1860999	RAF	**KL205**		†
08.02.45	Sgt William W.B. **Vaissiere**	RAF No. 1804677	RAF	**KJ134**		-
16.02.45	Sgt Denis **Garner**	RAF No. 1803120	RAF	**KJ147**		†
22.02.45	Sgt Alastair **Fraser**	RAF No. 1570107	RAF	**KJ142**		†
05.04.45	Sgt Oswald **Darlington**	RAF No. 1674723	RAF	**KJ351**		-
28.04.45	P/O Peter G. **Turner**	RAF No. 195574	RAF	**KJ342**		†
30.04.45	Sgt Peter **Clark**	RAF No. 1860201	RAF	**KJ183**		-
18.05.45	P/O Thomas **Wood**	RAF No. 163354	RAF	**KJ161**		†
28.07.45	Sgt Peter **Bosworth**	RAF No. 1608830	RAF	**KJ338**		†
20.09.45	Sgt Raymond C.B. **Mansfield**	RAF No. 1627541	RAF	**KL302**		-

Total: 12

KL328/14 is one of ten known unpainted Thunderbolts to have been issued to 73 OTU. *(Andrew Thomas)*

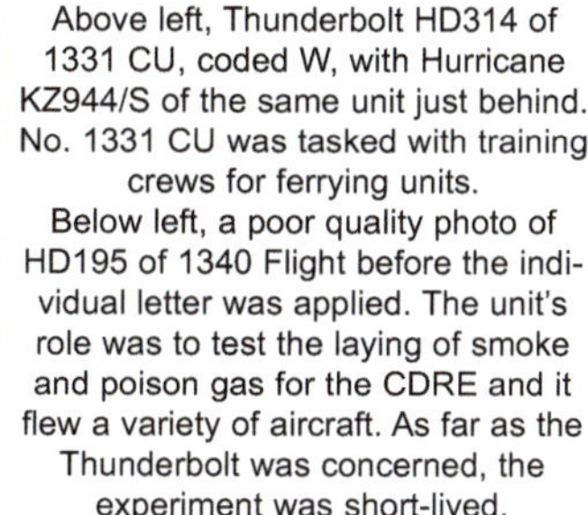

Above left, Thunderbolt HD314 of 1331 CU, coded W, with Hurricane KZ944/S of the same unit just behind. No. 1331 CU was tasked with training crews for ferrying units.
Below left, a poor quality photo of HD195 of 1340 Flight before the individual letter was applied. The unit's role was to test the laying of smoke and poison gas for the CDRE and it flew a variety of aircraft. As far as the Thunderbolt was concerned, the experiment was short-lived.

WITH THE MISCELLANEOUS UNITS

Due to a lack of records, the movement cards having been destroyed at the end of the war, it is difficult to know with certainty with which units the Thunderbolt Mk.II flew, except for those already mentioned. What it is known is that the Check & Conversion Flight (CCF) at Mauripur used some Mk.Is between May and September 1944. It was then re-named 1331 Conversion Unit and re-located to Risalpur. It was formed at first to train crews for ferrying duties, hence the use of several Thunderbolts of both marks. Regarding the Mk.II, HD214, KL243, KL295, KL310, KL333 and KL344 are known to have served with 1331 CU, but not necessarily at the same time. The Air Fighting Training Unit (AFTU) stationed at Armada Road used Mk.IIs as well (at least HD271 and KJ167). It was in charge of training Allied pilots in tactics practised by Japanese fighters and bombers in South East Asia and used a variety of aircraft types. The unit was disbanded in May 1945 to become the Tactical & Weapons Development Unit (TWDU) at the same location and was planned to have an establishment of Thunderbolts, Spitfires, Hurricanes, Beaufighters, Liberators and Austers (two of each), and three Mustangs (just being introduced in the theatre, hence the extra aircraft). As far as the Thunderbolt was concerned, however, only a trace of KJ167 (ex-AFTU) could be found. This unit was eventually disbanded on 30 November 1945. Less conventional is the use of two Thunderbolts (HD191 and HD195/F) with No. 1340 Flight. Formed on 25 September 1944 at Sulur as a Special Duty Flight, it was initially established with two Vultee Vengeances and later reinforced with Thunderbolts and Mosquitos. Its role was to test the laying of smoke and poison gas for the Chemical Defence Research Establishment (CDRE). The period during which the Thunderbolts were on strength is not known, but only the Vengeance type was still on charge when the unit disbanded. Otherwise, many Maintenance Units (MU), Repair & Salvage Units (RSU) or Ferry units (such as Ferry Control, Staging Post or Ferry Unit) used a number of Mk.IIs until the withdrawal of the type. Several accidents were recorded:

Date	Pilot	S/N	Origin	Serial	Code	Unit	Fate
28.11.44	F/O Cecil T. **ROBINSON**	RAF No. 147191	RAF	**KJ188**		320 MU	-
01.02.45	F/L Thomas **NESBITT**	RAF No. 119134	RAF	**KJ300**		308 MU	-
20.03.45	F/O Angus L. **CLARKE**	CAN./ J.87644	RCAF	**KL232**		9 FU	-
03.05.45	W/O Thomas **CARTER**	CAN./ R.113912	RCAF	**HD277**		1 CMU	-
08.06.45	W/O Harold T.B. **TAYLOR**	AUS. 421770	RAAF	**HD279**		308 MU	-
21.07.45	F/L Thomas B.O. **EVANS**	RAF No. 186109	RAF	**KJ167**		T&WDU	-
27.07.45	Sgt Sidney **NEWTON**	RAF No. 1802988	RAF	**KL255**		9 FU	†
20.08.45	F/L Paul E. **WELCH**	RAF No. 155210	RAF	**KL313**		36 SP	-
04.09.45	F/Sgt George B. **MACHIN**	RAF No. 1624903	RAF	**HD290**		36 SP	†
19.09.45	W/O Eddy E. **BUCK**	AUS. 409984	RAF	**HD256**		209 SP	-
10.10.45	*Ground accident*	-	-	**KL321**		59 SP	-
23.02.46	*Ground accident*	-	-	**KL227**		308 MU	-
04.03.46	S/L Jack **TURTON**	RAF No. 124816	RAF	**KJ213**		390 MU	†
14.03.46	*Ground accident**	-	-	**KL168**		132 RSU	-
	*Ground accident**	-	-	**KL264**		132 RSU	-
	*Ground accident**	-	-	**KL849**		132 RSU	-

Struck by Spitfire TZ191. KL168, Cat.AC but not repaired, KL264 and KL849 Cat.E and SOC.

Thunderbolt KJ284 is known to have flown for 3 TAF's Communication Squadron, a unit that used a great variety aircraft from the Tiger Moth to the Thunderbolt and up to the Dakota and Wellington. The use of a Hurricane or Thunderbolt was usually by a high-ranking officer or for high-speed courier flights. Like many liaison aircraft, no individual letter was worn.

IN MEMORIAM

Thunderbolt Mk. II

Name	Service No	Rank	Age	Origin	Date	Serial
BELLISLE, Joseph Louis Alphonse Roland	CAN./ J.20225	F/L	*n/k*	RCAF	12.02.45	KJ263
BOSWORTH, Peter	RAF No. 1608830	RAF	20	RAF	28.07.45	KJ338
BULLIMORE, Kenneth	RAF No. 1623877	F/Sgt	21	RAF	27.03.45	KJ136
BUTLER, Douglas Edward	RAF No.1615752	F/Sgt	22	RAF	10.09.45	KL189
BROWN, Sydney Walter	CAN./ J.20638	F/L	23	RCAF	07.05.45	HD217
CAMBRIDGE, Thomas Hudson	AUS. 410213	W/O	21	RAAF	21.12.44	KJ232
CATTELL, Edwin Annesley	RAF No. 700912	F/Sgt	20	RAF	17.03.45	KJ210
CHANEY, George Edwin	RAF No. 1318137	W/O	24	RAF	30.08.45	KJ356
CRAWSHAY-FRY, Peter William	RAF No. 181944	F/O	*n/k*	RAF	23.11.45	KJ226
FRASER, Alastair	RAF No. 1570107	Sgt	21	RAF	22.02.45	KJ142
GARNER, Denis	RAF No. 1803120	RAF	21	RAF	16.02.45	KJ147
GRADY, Donald Oliver	RAF No. 1607363	F/Sgt	21	RAF	14.04.45	KJ192
HALL, Martyn Bruce	SAAF No. 328370V	Lt	*n/k*	SAAF	10.02.45	HD252
HANSON, Jeffrey Graydon	RAF No. 55136	F/O	22	RAF	31.10.45	KL179
HARDY, Ian Griffiths	AUS. 420880	W/O	21	RAAF	17.11.44	HD298
HIDGEON, Peter William	RAF No. 1605075	Sgt	20	RAF	16.06.45	KJ293
HUBBLE, Michael Wintworth	RAF No. 49742	S/L	27	RAF	17.04.45	KL194
JACK, Russell Stuart	AUS. 410340	P/O	22	RAAF	21.04.45	KL231
JAMES, John Howard Frank	RAF No. 1339604	W/O	24	RAF	02.10.44	KL286
JONES, Emrys Ifan Huw	RAF No. 1379211	W/O	23	RAAF	05.09.44	HD283
KEIGHTLEY, Malcolm Clair	AUS. 416968	W/O	22	RAAF	24.04.45	KJ321
KENT, Frederick George	RAF No. 181419	F/O	21	RAF	12.08.45	KL222
LANSDOWN, Desmond William Burt	RAF No. 184368	F/O	21	RAF	10.02.45	KJ185
MACDONALD, Ian	RAF No. 1570587	F/Sgt	22	RAF	09.07.46	KL211
MACHIN, George Brian	RAF No. 1624203	F/Sgt	21	RAF	04.09.45	HD290
MACKENZIE, Roy	RAF No. 1393402	W/O	*n/k*	RAF	25.01.45	HD281
MURRAY, Douglas Shirley	RAF No. 1603065	F/Sgt	21	RAF	12.07.45	KL260
NEATE, Robert Spencer	RAF No. 1801115	F/Sgt	*n/k*	RAF	09.07.45	KJ252
NEWTON, Sydney	RAF No. 1802988	F/Sgt	23	RAF	27.07.45	KL255
O'NEILL, John Gerald	RAF No. 1439445	W/O	22	RAF	05.01.45	HD184
PHILLIPS, Denis Robert	RAF No. 1317412	F/Sgt	22	RAF	05.03.45	KJ227
RATTENBURY, Arthur Thomas	RAF No. 1804463	Sgt	23	RAF	24.02.45	KJ128
REES, Ronald Leonard	RAF No. 177417	F/O	25	RAF	01.02.45	KJ179
SMALL, John Roger Colston	RAF No. 1860999	Sgt	22	RAF	30.01.45	KL205
STEWART, George Alexander	CAN./ C.90340	F/O	27	RCAF	02.06.45	KL174
TURNER, Peter Gledden	RAF No. 195574	P/O	*n/k*	RAF	28.04.45	KJ342
TURTON, Jack	RAF No. 124816	S/L	*n/k*	RAF	04.03.46	KJ213
WATERS, Victor Alexander	RAF No. 1605509	Sgt	20	RAF	31.10.44	HD264
WATTS, Peter Raymond	RAF No. 1324711	W/O	23	RAF	08.11.45	KL259
WESTGARTH, Donald Dudley	AUS. 413463	P/O	23	RAAF	25.04.45	KJ325
WHITE, Arthur Alfred	AUS. 432912	F/Sgt	20	RAAF	13.01.45	KJ169
WOOD, Thomas	RAF No. 163354	P/O	25	RAF	18.05.45	KJ161

Total: 42

Australia: 7, Canada: 3, South Africa: 1, United Kingdom: 31

n/k: not known

Republic Thunderbolt Mk. II KJ140
No. 30 Squadron
Jumchar (India), December 1944

Republic Thunderbolt Mk. II KJ302
No. 42 Squadron
Meiktila (Burma), summer 1945

Republic Thunderbolt Mk. II KL882
No. 60 Squadron
Tanjore (India), summer 1945

Republic Thunderbolt Mk. II HD185
No. 81 Squadron
Java (NEI), late 1945

Republic Thunderbolt Mk. II HD295
No. 146 Squadron
Kumbhirgram (India), October 1944

Republic Thunderbolt Mk. II KJ283
No. 261 Squadron
Squadron Leader R.H. Fletcher
Wanjing (India), 1944-1945

SQUADRONS! - The series

1   The Supermarine Spitfire Mk VI
2   The Republic Thunderbolt Mk I
3   The Supermarine Spitfire Mk V in the Far East
4   The Boeing Fortress Mk I
5   The Supermarine Spitfire Mk XII
6   The Supermarine Spitfire Mk VII
7   The Supermarine Spitfire F. 21
8   The Handley-Page Halifax Mk I
9   The Forgotten Fighters
10   The NA Mustang IV in Western Europe
11   The NA Mustang IV over the Balkans and Italy
12   The Supermarine Spitfire Mk XVI - *The British*
13   The Martin Marauder Mk I
14   The Supermarine Spitfire Mk VIII in the Southwest Pacific - *The British*
15   The Gloster Meteor F.I & F.III
16   The NA Mitchell - *The Dutch, Poles and French*
17   The Curtiss Mohawk
18   The Curtiss Kittyhawk Mk II
19   The Boulton Paul Defiant - *day and night fighter*
20   The Supermarine Spitfire Mk VIII in the Southwest Pacific - *The Australians*
21   The Boeing Fortress Mk II & Mk III
22   The Douglas Boston and Havoc - *The Australians*
23   The Republic Thunderbolt Mk II
24   The Douglas Boston and Havoc - *Night fighters*
25   The Supermarine Spitfire Mk V - *The Eagles*
26   The Hawker Hurricane - *The Canadians*
27   The Supermarine Spitfire Mk V - *The 'Bombay' squadrons*
28   The Consolidated Liberator - *The Australians*
29   The Supermarine Spitfire Mk XVI - *The Dominions*
30   The Supermarine Spitfire Mk V - *The Belgian and Dutch squadrons*
31   The Supermarine Spitfire Mk V - *The New-Zealanders*
32   The Supermarine Spitfire Mk V - *The Norwegians*
33   The Brewster Buffalo
34   The Supermarine Spitfire Mk II - *The Foreign squadrons*
35   The Martin Marauder Mk II
36   The Supermarine Spitfire Mk V - *The Special Reserve squadrons*
37   The Supermarine Spitfire Mk XIV - *The Belgian and Dutch squadrons*
38   The Supermarine Spitfire Mk II - *The Rhodesian, Dominion & Eagle squadrons*
39   The Douglas Boston and Havoc - *Intruders*
40   The North American Mustang Mk III over Italy and the Balkans (Pt-1)
41   The Bristol Brigand
42   The Supermarine Spitfire Mk V - *The Australians*
43   The Hawker Typhoon - *The Rhodesian squadrons*
44   The Supermarine Spitfire F.22 & F.24
45   The Supermarine Spitfire Mk IX - *The Belgian and Dutch squadrons*
46   The North American & CAC Mustang - *The RAAF*
47   The Westland Whirlwind
48   The Supermarine Spitfire Mk XIV - *The British squadrons*
49   The Supermarine Spitfire Mk I - *The beginning (the Auxiliary squadrons)*
50   The Hawker Tempest Mk V - *The New Zealanders*
51   The Last of the Long-Range Biplane Flying Boats
52   The Supermarine Spitfire Mk IX - *The Former Canadian Homefront squadrons*
53   The Hawker Hurricane Mk I & Mk II - *The Eagle squadrons*
54   The Hawker biplane fighters
55   The Supermarine Spitfire Mk IX - *The Auxiliary squadrons*
56   The Hawker Typhoon - *The Canadian squadrons*
57   The Douglas SBD - *New Zealand and France*
58   The Forgotten Patrol Seaplanes
59   The Dutch Fighter Squadrons - *Nos. 322 & 120 (NEI) Squadrons*
60   The Supermarine Spitfire - *The Australian Squadrons in Western Europe and the Med*
61   The Belgian Fighter Squadrons - *Nos. 349 & 350 Squadrons*
62   The Supermarine Spitfire Mk I - *The beginning (the Regular squadrons)*
63   The Hawker Typhoon - *The 'Fellowship of the Bellows' squadrons*
64   The North American Mustang Mk I & Mk II

Donald James Matthew BLAKESLEE DFC

Supermarine Spitfire Mk.VB EN951
No. 133 (Eagle) Squadron
Flight Lieutenant D. J. M. Blakeslee
CAN./J.4551
Gravesend (UK), August 1942

Charles Cuthbertson LEARMONTH DFC*

Douglas Boston Mk. III A28-9 (071-AL891)
No. 22 Squadron RAAF
Squadron Leader C. C. Learmonth
Aus. 385
Port Moresby (New Guinea), spring 1943

Hans Anton MAURENBRECHER

Curtiss P-40N-35-CU C3-360
No. 120 (NEI) Squadron
Major H. Maurenbrecher
Biak (New Guinea), 1943-1945

Roland Prosper BEAMONT DSO* DFC*

Hawker Tempest Mk.V JN751
No. 150 Wing
Wing Commander R. P. Beamont
RAF No. 21819
Bradwell Bay (UK), April 1944

Ronald Thomas SUSANS DSO DFC

North American P-51D-23-NT A68-724
No. 77 squadron, RAAF
Squadron Leader R. T. Susans
O4361
Bofu (Japan), 1947

James Henry LACEY DFM*

Supermarine Spitfire Mk.XIV RN135
No. 17 Squadron
Squadron Leader J. H. Lacey
RAF No. 112709
Seletar (Singapore), autumn 1945

Introducing's RAF In Combat and Bravo Bravo Aviation's collection of highly-detailed and historically accurate, high-quality aviation prints.
For more information on available prints, please visit :

www.raf-in-combat.com   or

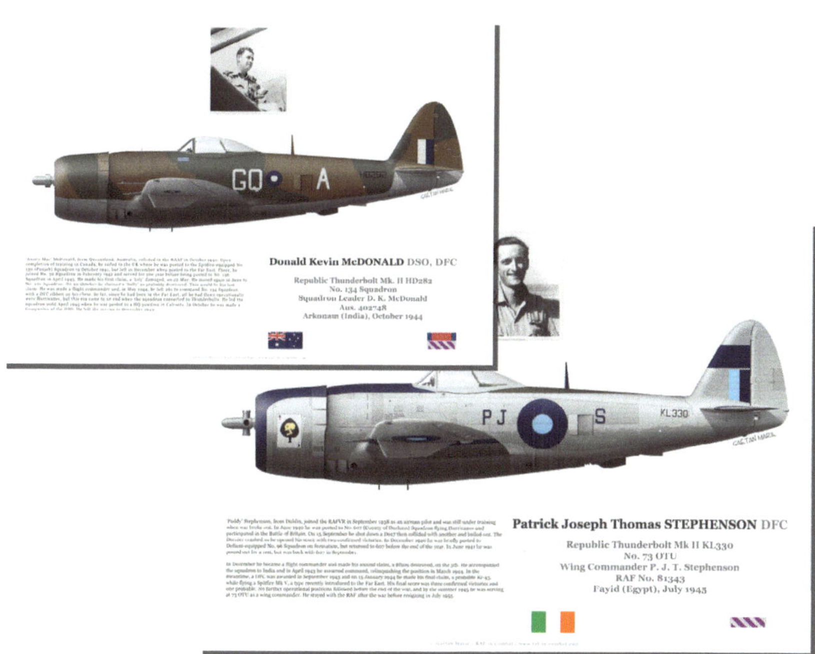

Donald Kevin McDONALD DSO, DFC

Republic Thunderbolt Mk. II HD282
No. 134 Squadron
Squadron Leader D. K. McDonald
Aus. 402748
Arkonam (India), October 1944

Patrick Joseph Thomas STEPHENSON DFC

Republic Thunderbolt Mk II KL330
No. 73 OTU
Wing Commander P. J. T. Stephenson
RAF No. 81343
Fayid (Egypt), July 1945

Prints available for this book:

PL-015: P.J.T. Stephenson
PL-047: D.K. McDonald
PL-173: F.R. Carey
PL-174: R.D. May
PL-175: A.J. McGregor